# FOLLOW IS A VERB

## PRACTICING THE HABITS OF JESUS TOGETHER

COURTNEY HIRSCHEIDER

LEAFWOOD PUBLISHERS
an imprint of Abilene Christian University Press

***Follow Is a Verb***
*Practicing the Habits of Jesus Together*

LEAFWOOD PUBLISHERS
*an imprint of Abilene Christian University Press*



ISBN 978-1-68426-364-6 | LCCN 2025007444

Printed in the United States of America



Library of Congress Cataloging-in-Publication Data

Names: Hirscheider, Courtney author
Title: Follow is a verb : practicing the habits of Jesus together / Courtney Hirscheider.
Description: Abilene, Texas : Leafwood Publishers, [2025] | Includes bibliographical references.
Identifiers: LCCN 2025007444 (print) | LCCN 2025007445 (ebook) | ISBN 9781684263646 paperback | ISBN 9781684268245 ebook
Subjects: LCSH: Christian life—Study and teaching
Classification: LCC BV4511 .H57 2025 (print) | LCC BV4511 (ebook) | DDC 248.4—dc23/eng/20250710
LC record available at https://lccn.loc.gov/2025007444
LC ebook record available at https://lccn.loc.gov/2025007445

Cover design by Molly von Borstel, Faceout Studio
Interior text design by Nord Compo

Leafwood Publishers is an imprint of Abilene Christian University Press
ACU Box 29138
Abilene, Texas 79699
1-877-816-4455
www.leafwoodpublishers.com

25 26 27 28 29 30 31 // 7 6 5 4 3 2 1

# Praise for
# Follow Is a Verb

"When it comes to spiritual formation, most of us need practical guidance, not just content explaining why it is needed. We need steps, practices, encouragement, and invitations. In *Follow Is a Verb*, Courtney does just that. She does not write as one who has arrived but one who is on the journey with us. This book belongs on the shelf next to Ruth Haley Barton and John Mark Comer. It is that good."

—**Josh Ross**, pastor and author

"Courtney Hirscheider's passion for teaching the habits of Jesus has been contagious for our congregation. From new Christians to shepherds, our members are growing deeper in their relationship with God and as disciple makers by applying these practices in life together."

—**Jonathan Storment**, pastor and author

"As a builder for many years, we had the opportunity to erect complex structural systems. When we would ask the engineer who designed a particular building how to hold it all together during construction before the final pieces came together, they would respond, 'That's means and methods! We aren't responsible for that; you are.' What Courtney has done is lead us through the 'means and methods' our Designer provides for building the life he envisions for each of us."

—**Jimmy Cone**, shepherd, Pleasant Valley Church of Christ, vice chairman of the board, Harding University

"Spiritual growth is best when pursued in community where we have encouragement and accountability. So, whether it's in a Sunday school class or in your home with a group of friends, consider reading *Follow Is a Verb* to practice the habits of Jesus together."

—**Sara Gaston Barton**, chaplain, editor, and author of *A Woman Called*

# CONTENTS

# HOW TO USE THIS STUDY

I WAS LESS THAN A WEEK OLD when my parents first took me to church. I was taught the rights and wrongs, memorized famous verses, named the apostles, and learned the books of the Bible in order. And more importantly, I learned that people at church were an extended family who loved me.

But I found myself in adulthood, like many I go to church with now and many I grew up with, doing and doing for God but not really knowing him. I knew something must be missing. The foundation of love and commitment I experienced growing up in church kept me from walking away and, in a way, it was what led me to search for more.

It wasn't until I discovered the depth and beauty of practicing the habits of Jesus that I actively, passionately, and wholeheartedly put my entire life and heart in his hands. It was like scales falling off my eyes as I began to see and experience my faith more clearly. The practices we will discover and dig into in this study helped *following Jesus* take new meaning in my life. *Follow* became a verb for me, and it has changed everything.

**Read and Meditate on**
Matthew 8:23–27

## Sleeping on the Boat

In this passage Matthew, a disciple of Jesus, describes what must have been a harrowing scene. Jesus, the Son of God, is traveling in a small boat with those who have chosen to follow him and learn from him what it means to be a disciple. A furious storm is building around them, and Jesus is sound asleep as the disciples' anxieties and fears continue to rise.

Jesus is calm enough to rest because he knows the Father is in control and has given him authority over the storm. He can sleep in the boat because he knows God well enough to trust him with everything. This is a lesson the disciples will learn repeatedly as they follow him. By observing the life and teachings of Jesus, we too can learn how to know God well enough to trust him with everything. When practiced over a lifetime, the lessons he teaches, such as how to listen, obey, pray, value Scripture, rest, and love one another, form us into people who are more like him.

Training your soul through the practices we see in the life of Jesus is much like training your heart through cardiovascular exercise. The more time you spend training your physical heart through exercise, the more quickly your body can return to a resting heart rate when you stop. Similarly, the more time you spend in the presence of God, the more quickly you will be able to return to your resting soul rate—the place where you slow down, listen well to God and others, and feel at peace. This is where you find yourself more open to receiving the love of God and giving it more freely.

So, can you sleep on the boat? Do you want to? Hopefully this study will help you do just that. Our goal together will be to help you connect with God in new ways and trust him more deeply with your past, present, and future. When we trust God completely, we let go of control, pressure, guilt, pride, and distraction and accept the kingdom life God promises to us, his sons and daughters.

This book is not an all-inclusive manual for spiritual formation. It is a jumping-off point. It will introduce concepts and practices that have been written about and studied for centuries in an accessible format. It will focus on *practicing* the habits of Jesus more than *learning* about them. This book does not claim to be breaking new ground. We will start simply by looking at what Jesus actually did and then introduce some of the best ways to apply those practices, practices that other Christians have lived into and written about for the past two thousand years. So, prayerfully gather your people (three to six is ideal), and let's get started.

**Lesson Guide**

Each lesson, except the introduction and the final lesson, is meant to last two weeks. This allows each practice to be introduced and tried in week one and practiced more deeply in week two.

The slow pace is intentional, leaning more into applying the practices than reading and discussing them. The second week should lend itself to discussions while living life together, such as eating a meal, traveling to an event, or enjoying recreational activities like hiking, shopping, fishing, or grabbing coffee. This is encouraged and helps the group take on more of the natural rhythms of life-on-life relationships modeled by Jesus.

Each chapter also contains resources for going deeper. These are meant to be engaged as part of the study and as supplements to the reading. Direct links to these resources can be found at www.

pvcc.org/resources. As you go, remember that every season of life and stage of discipleship brings unique challenges, and no practice is a mandate. Each should be viewed as an invitation meant to be received in humility and grace.

The tools in this guide are just that: tools. They are not the only way to seek God but resources to help you cut through the routine, habits, and baggage you may have acquired and get back to simply knowing God better. As Gerald Sittser says in his book *Water from a Deep Well*, "We will never be able to love, pray, think, feel, work, meditate, fast or even die our way into a deeper spiritual life if we rely on human effort . . . because in Jesus Christ God has already made His way to us . . . we are recipients of grace, beloved of God. Prodigals welcomed home."[1]

# Introduction

## DISCIPLE-MAKING AND DESIRE

WORDS MATTER—ESPECIALLY WORDS that define us. The words we use shape how we see ourselves and our expectations for ourselves and others. Churches often overuse and overbrand themselves with words like *disciple, disciple making*, and even the word *Christian* itself. The intent is solid, but the result of calling everyone who shows up a disciple is that the term can become diluted and weakened and not make much of a difference in an individual's daily life.

### Who Is a Disciple?

The noun *disciple* comes from the Latin word *discipulus*, which means student, learner, or follower. The word *discipline* can mean to study, learn, train, and apply a system of standards. It can also mean to teach or to guide lovingly.

The Hebrew word for disciple is *talmid*. This word stresses the relationship between rabbi (teacher or master) and disciple (student). A *talmid* of Jesus's day would give up his entire life to be with his teacher. The disciple didn't only seek to know what the teacher knew but also left everything to follow the teacher.

*Christian* was originally used as a negative term, making fun of the first followers of Jesus for being "little Christs."

When you think of the word *disciple,* is it synonymous with *Christian*? Are all Christians disciples? Can you be a disciple without being a disciple-maker?

For this book, we will define disciple and disciple-making as Jesus did in his call in Matthew 4:19: "Come, follow me," Jesus said, "and I will show you how to fish for people" (NLT).

- **Be with Jesus** (*Come, follow me*): Choose him. Abide in him. Slow down enough to hear his voice and practice being in his presence.
- **Become like Jesus** (*I will show you how*): Allow the Holy Spirit to transform your heart and help you become a person of deep love, a person to whom the teachings of Jesus are second nature. You will not get everything "right" all the time, but over time your will and your heart will become aligned with his.
- **Do what Jesus did** (*Fish for people*): What would Jesus do with your one and only life if he were walking around in your skin today? How would he interact with your neighbors and family, answer your emails, and connect in your community?

---

So the greatest issue facing the world today, with all its heartbreaking needs, is whether those who, by profession or culture, are identified as "Christians" will become disciples—students, apprentices, practitioners—of Jesus Christ, steadily learning from him how to live the life of the Kingdom of the Heavens into every corner of human existence.

—**Dallas Willard,** *The Great Omission*[1]

---

## Becoming a Disciple

Now that we have a practical definition of discipleship and disciple-making, let's move on to what Jesus thought was the most important part. In Matthew 22:36–40 (NLT), and also in Luke 10 and Mark 12, we find Jesus answering this very question:

> "Teacher, which is the most important commandment in the law of Moses?" Jesus replied, "'You must love the LORD your God with all your heart, all your soul, and all your mind.' This is the first and greatest commandment. A second is equally important: 'Love your neighbor as yourself.' The entire law and all the demands of the prophets are based on these two commandments."

**Read and Meditate on**
John 3:16; John 13:34–35; 1 Corinthians 13; 1 John 4:7–12

*Begin with Love*

The call to discipleship begins by simply responding to God's love for you and sharing it with others. One of the most famous verses in the Bible, John 3:16, says that *God loved* (us), *so he gave* (his son). Love is the foundation of the whole gospel. Jesus calls it the "new command" and the "greatest command" (John 13: 34; Matt. 22:38). Flip forward in your Bible a few more books, and John doubles down on this. In 1 John 4:8, he shares that we cannot even know God without love because "God is love."

Discipleship begins with the knowledge that *you* are deeply loved by God—you, right where you are. As you carry the brokenness you are working on and that you hope doesn't hurt anyone, you are loved. As you sit with the parts of yourself that no one sees and that you are trying to hide, you are loved. You are deeply loved, valued, and celebrated by God before even getting out of bed in the morning and doing a thing.

### *Continue in Love*

1 Corinthians 13 reminds us that all is lost if we are not walking in love. This chapter is familiar to anyone who has been to a Christian wedding, but it has taken on a much deeper meaning for me lately due to the prompting of preschoolers.

Our church building shares space with a private elementary school. For a few years, my office had a back door that led to a hallway where every day the preschool class walked through on their way to lunch. As they walked, they would recite 1 Corinthians 13. What a gift it was to me to almost daily hear these little voices proclaim these big truths. No matter what was going on in my day, I could not help but stop and listen to the wisdom they were sharing.

It doesn't matter how smart, talented, or hardworking we are, or even how great our faith is, if we do not love. If we are not living out a love that is patient, kind, and humble, it is all for nothing. I love Paul's language here so much that I bought a gong for my office to remind myself how I sound too much of the time when I am not leading with love (see verse 1).

### *The End Goal Is Love*

The apostle John begins to close his account of Jesus's life in John 13. The chapter describes Jesus's final private moments with his closest followers before he is handed over to be crucified. The end is near. He knows the struggles, fears, doubts, and persecutions they will all face, both immediately and throughout the rest of their lives, as they proclaim his good news to the world.

Instead of a sermon, in this crucial moment Jesus chose an object lesson. He surprised them all by taking the lowest role and washing their feet before the meal, again illustrating this new kind of sacrificial love. With their feet still damp from that physical lesson, he tells them, "A new command I give you: Love one another. As I have loved you, so you must love one another. By *this* everyone will know that you are my disciples, if you love one another" (John 13:34–35—emphasis mine).

Through foot washing, Jesus is preparing them for their final lesson in the kind of love he is talking about.

So, the beginning of discipleship is love, and the end is love. We begin by recognizing the love God has for each one of us as his children, and we respond to that love by following his son and being obedient to his commands (Matt. 28:20). We grow to embody that love, sharing it with everyone he puts in our lives. The whole life of a disciple is rooted in love, and the fruit of that love makes new disciples. Discipleship is *for* the sake of others.

So, how do we practically become people who love like this? How do we take Jesus more seriously every day? How do we move toward a relationship with him that goes beyond just something we do on Sunday mornings and the occasional service project while we wait for heaven? How do we become people who think, play, serve, worship, and, most importantly, share the gospel as Jesus did?

## Growing as a Disciple

Becoming a transformed disciple of King Jesus does not require a degree in theology or a complicated set of processes. But it does require practice. To follow God and share his love in a real, meaningful way, we must first love him. To love him, we must know him, and to know him, we must spend time with him.

God, in his goodness, gave us simple disciplines like silence, solitude, prayer, and fasting—practices modeled by Jesus that allow us to hear God's voice and be changed. He also gave us each other to walk together in relational discipleship, as Jesus did with the twelve.

Too many times in our churches, we focus on managing our sins in hopes of being obedient to Christ. James 3:7–8 reminds us, "All kinds of animals, birds, reptiles and sea creatures are being tamed and have been tamed by mankind, but no human being can tame the tongue. It is a restless evil, full of deadly poison." The wisdom offered here by Jesus's brother can be applied to all the sins we try to master through our will. We may succeed for a while, but in the end, without the Holy Spirit's transforming power in our hearts, we cannot become people who look more like Jesus.

The practices or spiritual disciplines that we see in the lives of Jesus and his earliest followers allow us to counter Satan's lies and isolation. They empower us to fight the spiritual battles in our neighborhoods and our hearts. They are not about doing more but about slowing down our pace of life to live in the grace of God.

These practices are simple, but the transformation is not magical or quick. The work of the Holy Spirit within us requires a lifelong commitment to the way of Jesus. As we mature in discipleship, we begin to see the world through his eyes and trust his vision as to what the good life is. And as we walk together in discipling communities, we continually sharpen each other (Prov. 27:17) and spur each other on (Heb. 10:24–25).

**Read and Meditate on**
Matthew 28:19–20

## Disciple-Making

Through the New Testament and church history, we know that those who walked with Jesus were changed. They lived drastically differently than the cultures around them. They were willing to die for their belief that Jesus was, in fact, the Son of God. But what if they had kept all of that to themselves? What if they had retreated inward, focusing solely on their relationship with God? Or what if those who heard their message decided that the great commission was just for the original audience and not a charge to be shared over and over across generations?

Jesus's last words to the eleven remaining disciples in Matthew 28 laid out the expectation of multiplication. Jesus is telling us that healthy spiritual formation looks outward. It is not content to go deeper with God and your best Christian friends. It is meant to prepare you to go into the world. As we grow as disciples, our hearts soften to care more deeply about our neighbors' physical and spiritual needs and act on that concern. Despite our backgrounds and history with God, we begin to truly see our brokenness and have real, Christlike empathy for the world around us. We want to multiply ourselves, helping others find the salvation and healing we have experienced as we grow in love, joy, peace, patience, kindness, goodness, faithfulness, gentleness, and self-control through the power of the Holy Spirit (Gal. 5:22–23).

Making disciples might sound like a challenge, a calling, or something you don't fully understand, but at its core, it is like giving food to someone starving. It reminds us how good the gospel really is and how it is good news for everyone. It will fill you with joy as you get a front-row seat to the life change made possible only by the power of the Holy Spirit. It will build your faith in new and life-giving ways.

But what are we called to multiply? What does a mature disciple look like? Pointing back to Matthew 28 and John 13:35, Jesus says we will be known by our love, we will have been baptized, and we will obey his teachings. To multiply ourselves as disciples, our lives must be something worth repeating. We must continually be growing as disciples ourselves.

### Desire

Maturing as a disciple begins with ordering your desires. It is not about a new set of rules and figuring out all you should and should not do. It is about aligning your heart with the will of God.

> God is trying to reorder our desires toward himself. God is not trying to limit our desires but to direct them back to a divine source.
>
> —**Jefferson Bethke and Jon Tyson,** *Fighting Shadows*[2]

Increasing the desire to know and love God has become the primary prayer I pray for myself, my husband, my children, the leaders of our church, and those closest to me. That is the foundation of the abundant life—not that we will find the right spouse, the right job, be healed from illness, or make wise decisions—it is knowing and loving God. The gift of being able to walk in a close, loving relationship with our Creator sets everything else in our life on a course for stability, peace, joy, and freedom from all the broken parts of our humanity that weigh us down.

**Read and Meditate on**
Jeremiah 29:10–14

*Freedom*

Jeremiah was a prophet of God who was born around 650 BC. His book includes history, biography, and prophecy, as well as a letter of encouragement from God to his people. The Israelites at that time were a nation in crisis. They were exiled to Babylon, living in and being discipled by a culture in submission to an earthly king. The Lord promised to bring them back home, but this restoration will take decades to come to fruition. In the meantime, God commissioned the prophet Jeremiah to send them a letter.

The prophet's words to them offer truth for us today. We may not be under a foreign government's control, but everywhere we turn, Satan is using someone or something to disciple us away from the way of Jesus. God wants to bring us all back from whatever captivity we have allowed ourselves to be stuck in—from addiction and greed to anxiety, pride, self-righteousness, and apathy. God has plans to prosper us. He is listening to our prayers and longs to free us from the brokenness we all experience, to give us a new, beautifully abundant life in Christ. He is waiting to answer our call for help. Do we truly want to be freed?

**Read and Meditate on**
Mark 10:46–52

*Rescue*

The blind beggar Bartimaeus sits by the side of the road, helpless and hopeless. We don't know how long he has been there, but we can imagine the desperation in his voice as he tries to get Jesus's attention on the noisy street. Those around tried to silence him, but Bartimaeus is not stopped. He has the kind of desperation that does not care what others think and does not act in line with what is expected. "Jesus," he cries out, "Son of David, have mercy on me!" Jesus hears his honesty and desperation above all other voices. And Jesus responds with the same question he's asking us as we approach him today: "What do you want me to do for you?" Place yourself on that road just outside the walls of Jericho. How would you answer Jesus?

**Read and Meditate on**
John 18:15–27; John 21:15–19

*Restoration*

Peter denied Jesus three times before his crucifixion. Jesus told Peter it would happen, but Peter did not believe it was possible. Until it happened. Peter was no doubt wrecked, confused, full of shame and fear, and not knowing where to turn. Then Jesus, in his goodness, gave Peter three chances to redeem himself.

Jesus asked Peter three times, "Do you love me?" Not, "Do you love preaching and teaching?" or "Do you love these miracles and feeling good when we help people together?" He didn't say, "Do you love this community of brothers and sisters I've given you?" He asked instead, "Do *you* love *me*?" Are you willing to turn your life upside down due to that love? Are you willing to love that deeply? Is following him what you desire most?

***

> God wants to fulfill our desires with what truly satisfies. God is not afraid of our desires, he is saddened by the weakness of them. He wants us to hunger for more and refuse to settle for less.
>
> **—Jefferson Bethke and Jon Tyson,** *Fighting Shadows*[3]

Whether you are new to following Christ or have been a Christian a long time, a deep, personal relationship with a being you cannot physically see or touch can seem elusive at times. Maybe you find yourself looking around and wondering why belief and desire for God seem to come more naturally for those around you. Maybe it seems like this level of spirituality is something other people have tapped into, but maybe that's just not your personality. Maybe you have strong passions and desires that betray you at every turn and leave you feeling anything but godly.

Our desires are from God. He created us in his image to be creators, to have passions, to strive for more. But when we let our desires run wild apart from God, everything goes sideways. Our desires lead us to places we never thought we would go and into sin patterns that begin to take a toll on our lives and relationships. Even desires that don't result in sin can leave us distracted and off-mission as they begin to take over our thoughts, schedules, and conversations. When our desires are left unchecked, it can become difficult to imagine a life where our greatest desire is a relationship with our Creator. We become restless because, deep down, we know that what we are chasing will never truly satisfy.

In his book *The Holy Longing*, Ronald Rolheiser says, "Your restlessness is the beginning of your spiritual journey."[4] We are infinite beings living in a finite world. To overcome this tension, we must lean into it.

---

Jesus answered her, "If you knew the gift of God and who it is that asks you for a drink, you would have asked him and he would have given you living water." (John 4:10)

On the last and greatest day of the festival, Jesus stood and said in a loud voice, "Let anyone who is thirsty come to me and drink. Whoever believes in me, as Scripture has said, rivers of living water will flow from within them." (John 7:37–38)

---

Life with God is the only thing that can truly satisfy the deepest longings of our hearts. It is the living water that counters the lies which disorder our desires and drive our lives into chaos, loneliness, addiction, apathy, and depression. Growing in your desire for God and the way you seek him can change how you feel about yourself, how you relate to others, and how you fundamentally live this life you have been given.

**Individual Practice**

Spend time in prayer asking the Holy Spirit to increase your desire for God—to know him more and feel his presence more tangibly in your life. Set an alarm right now to remind you to ask every day for the next week that God will reveal himself and his love for you more and more. Pray that you will seek him over everything else.

Pray for each member of your group by name.

### In Community

*Group Discussion*

1. What stood out to you in the chapter and/or the Scripture readings?
2. Pause on each of these and consider or discuss your honest answer to the following questions:

   - Is *he* what we really want?
   - Do we really love *him*?
   - Do we really know him enough to answer those questions at all?
   - Are we seeking him with all our hearts and submitting our will to align with his?
   - Do we also have the desire to look outward? To follow Jesus in loving the world enough to share his good news with it?

*Group Prayer Prompt*

End this week's discussion by praying as a group (each person taking a line or two) this prayer from Trevor Hudson in his book *Seeking God*.[5]

> Lord Jesus Christ,
> Your good news has found its way into my heart. Thank you for the divine life that your own life, death, and resurrection make possible for me today. I have caught a glimpse of what this life looks like in your own life and I yearn to know it for myself. Today I turn toward you, trusting that this is your vision for my life here on earth. As I learn what it means to seek you and the life you give, May your Spirit show me my next step.

**Go Deeper**

*Sacred Rhythms,* Ruth Haley Barton, Chapter 1

*The Good and Beautiful God: Falling in Love with the God Jesus Knows,* James Bryan Smith

*The Holy Longing: The Search for a Christian Spirituality,* Ronald Rolheiser

*Fighting Shadows,* Jefferson Bethke and Jon Tyson

For direct links, visit www.pvcc.org/resources.

# Practice One

## COMMUNITY

THIS STUDY WAS CREATED FOR a community, and so that is where we will begin. Take some time with the readings before diving in to the material in this chapter. Spoiler alert: We will do this with each new discipline, so please don't skip it.

**Read and Meditate on**
Matthew 12:48–49; Luke 2:41–52; John 1:35–43; Acts 2:42–47; 1 Peter 4:8–10

I've always prided myself on being efficient. I'm a doer, an achiever, a plate spinner, and man, do I stay busy. Even as a kid, maybe in the fourth or fifth grade, I remember being called out in a Wednesday night Bible class for talking while the lesson was being taught and not paying attention. I confidently repeated back the lesson points verbatim to the teacher to justify my disrespect and prove that "I can do it all at once."

My college roommate was the complete opposite in this regard, and it wasn't until I spent a lot of time with her that I realized maybe I was the one missing something. She always had the time to sit and talk with someone and was always willing to be interrupted to connect with someone, meet a need, or just experience something new and unexpected. And while this drove me crazy, I began to see that in practicing community, she often looked more like Jesus than I did.

### Jesus in Community

The Gospel of Luke is the only place in the Bible where we see a detailed picture of the community that raised Jesus. As he closes the second chapter of his Gospel, Luke sets the scene of his rabbi as a twelve-year-old boy. Jesus and his family have been together with their community at the Festival of the Passover in Jerusalem, and they are now traveling home. Jesus is thought to be among the friends and relatives, but after a day of travel, his parents realize he's missing. After three stressful days of searching, they finally find that he has stayed back in the temple, learning, teaching, and experiencing God in community.

Both sides of this story illustrate a life deeply rooted in community. From the travel plan to the choice Jesus made to stay behind, we see that being a disciple is not an individualistic activity. We see from his parents' trust in their traveling companions to the importance he placed on what was happening at the temple that discipleship is a communal process where people learn and grow together.

As Jesus began his years of adult ministry, he started with a call to community. The invitation was simply, "Follow me," but the meaning was much deeper. Jesus was asking them to change the course of their lives, to walk alongside him, to eat, sleep, and live together in a discipling community. The disciples' choice to belong and invest in community rerouted their entire lives and changed the course of human history forever.

The introduction to Practicing the Way courses beautifully articulates why community is so vital to our spiritual lives:

> As we practice the way of Jesus, we need partners for the journey, a community to help us along the way. Jesus invites all who follow him to be a part of a new family. This family of God is not a social club or a group of friends who look, think, and talk similarly but a community of apprentices following Jesus's way of life. And despite the work it takes, the fights we will endure, and the learning we will do along the way, together we're figuring out how to be with Jesus, become like him, and do what he did.[1]

### The Ache

The early Christians had community down. In a defense of Christianity written in AD 125, second-century Athenian philosopher Aristides lists a number of characteristics he saw that made the early Christians stand out. In particular he said, "If anyone among them comes into want while they themselves have nothing to spare, they fast for two or three days for him. In this way, they can supply any poor man with the food he needs." This was a community that not only knew the felt needs of each other but regularly acted on them in sacrificial love.[2]

Fast-forward a couple thousand years, and at least in the West, we are more digitally connected than ever before. The entire world and everyone we've ever known or wish to know can be summoned, or at least viewed, in an instant with the little rectangle in our pocket. And still, the rates of loneliness climb higher and higher. *Connectivity* is way up, but *community* is way down. Our culture has settled for a dim, digital replacement for what God intended our lives together to look like. And the results are showing their ugly heads in our collective mental health.

Writing in the *Harvard Business Review* in 2017, physician and former US Surgeon General Vivek Murthy noted, "During my years caring for patients, the most common pathology I saw was not heart disease or diabetes; it was loneliness." Noting that rates of loneliness in the United States have doubled since the 1980s, Dr. Murthy called the condition "a growing health epidemic" and pointed to research showing that "loneliness and weak social connections are associated with a reduction in lifespan similar to that caused by smoking fifteen cigarettes a day and even greater than that associated with obesity."[3]

Secular society is crying out for community. We saw this in so many ways during the Covid-19 pandemic in 2020, and it seemed for a minute that after being isolated for so long, human beings might make a real and lasting shift back to deeper and healthier connections when they were finally given the opportunity to reengage. But when the world opened back up and masks were removed, we went back to business as usual. We quickly filled our schedules back up, but we were too busy to notice the people around us. Now we find ourselves just as busy as we were pre-pandemic but with the added option to facilitate many of our jobs, gatherings, and meetings from a screen within the isolation of our homes.

We ache for deeper connections, but we lack the commitment, courage, and willingness to be transparent. We don't want people up in our business telling us what to do or making our lives too messy. We have a family for that, right? Most of us have jobs, hobbies, and community commitments, and who has time to have a neighbor over when you have all that plus school to study for, kids' activities five nights a week, or aging parents to check on? It often feels like we are just barely keeping our heads above water. When we finally come up for air in the week or in our season of life, we are tired, and the last thing we want to do is give that time away.

The call to create a community in our busy culture can seem incredibly daunting, not to mention the fear, awkwardness, and insecurity wrapped up in reaching out and intentionally pulling others into your circle. But at the end of the day, we are so lonely that it's killing us. Our world is hungry for a better option that only Jesus can give.

Practicing community and hospitality the way Jesus modeled is not easy. It requires sacrifice and time on our part. It also requires humility and vulnerability, emotional investments that can be just as hard as the physical energy and time required. But if we will trust Jesus in this, and if we will lead with love, we can discover the beautiful invitation he is trying to extend.

### Christian Community

There are all types of communities being built in our society to fight the loneliness epidemic, from CrossFit to the golf course to your local school or book club. But Jesus had something deeper in mind. When we follow Jesus throughout the Gospels, we see him life-on-life with his disciples. They ate together, prayed and worshipped together, traveled together, learned together, rested together, supported each other, got frustrated with each other, and everything in between. And eventually, they chose each other.

The twelve were radically different in personality and political leanings. They were not just an easy bunch of friends who naturally clicked and enjoyed hanging out. When they said yes to following Jesus, it was a yes they had to recommit to over and over. This took great patience, love, and commitment.

> They devoted themselves to the apostles' teaching and to fellowship, to the breaking of bread and to prayer. . . . All the believers were together and had everything in common. . . . Every day they continued to meet together in the temple courts. They broke bread in their homes and ate together with glad and sincere hearts. (Acts 2:42–47)

The early church in Acts 2 was a family in the most real and positive way. When they spoke about themselves, they used the Greek word *adelphoi* (brother or sister) to describe each other, and they meant it. They were multiethnic and multiracial, they honored and respected women, and they took care of the poor and vulnerable in ways unheard of in any culture up to that point in history.

The church exploded with growth. This was largely due to the deep, sacrificially loving community mindset where the needs and rights of the group as a whole were valued over the needs and rights of the individual. This mindset is a huge challenge in our Western culture, but it was even more radical in Jesus's time.

Jesus's definition of family as "whoever does God's will" in Matthew 12 went against all sorts of social norms and expectations. Your bloodline was what mattered in the Roman world. Parents took care of their children, and children were expected to return the favor. Jewish rabbis took this a step further by making this practice legally enforceable (Mishnah Kiddushin 1:7). It was also unthinkable in Jesus's day for a rabbi to teach women alongside men, and yet there they are. Women were present all through the gospel story and early church history, learning, serving, and leading alongside their brothers.

Jesus is not suggesting we ignore the needs of our biological families. He is instead drilling down on the importance of Christian community in the life of a disciple and how that outweighs ethnicity, gender, bloodline, personality, interests, abilities, and skill sets. Jesus is saying that *whoever* does God's will is welcome, even if they are super annoying.

And the result of trusting him enough to stick it out and actually live that way, being committed, accountable, patient, and loving to one another, moves us toward the agape love of God. It gets us closer to the heart of God who created us out of an overflowing of his relational, self-giving love. We were created to mirror that love as image-bearers of God. Over a lifetime and through the power of the Holy Spirit, that love will transform us as disciples, healing and being healed in community.

### Hospitality versus Entertainment

Walk through the book of Luke, and you'll generally find Jesus at a meal, leaving a meal, or going to a meal. Sometimes he's the host, sometimes he's a guest, and sometimes he's invited himself. But he's always connecting around a table. The gospel spread in the first century through radically ordinary hospitality, which still rings true today.

Church people tend to do the food part of hospitality pretty well. When did you last show up for a planned event at a church and food was not involved? It's almost a given to the point that on our church staff, the decision is not *when* to provide food but more often when *not* to have food.

However, one thing that is easy to miss is the difference between hospitality and entertainment. Hospitality is all about how you make other people feel. Entertaining is all about yourself. When we confuse the two, following Jesus can seem like an impossible burden. We think that to practice hospitality, we have to create environments and meals that will end up in social media feeds the next morning.

> Hospitality is about providing a place for God's Spirit to move, where people feel loved and welcomed, and God's Spirit can work in their lives. Hospitality is a very ordinary business, but in its ordinariness, it's real work. Your table is a sacred place, no matter what it looks like. Entertainment is about exclusion, about inviting the in-crowd. Hospitality is about inclusion; it's an open invitation. Hospitality means the love of the stranger and the outsider. Entertainment is about performance and what you can do. Hospitality is about service and tangible love expressed as welcome over a meal.
>
> **—John Mark Comer,** "Radically Ordinary Hospitality"[4]

The book *The Gospel Comes with a House Key* is a must-read on this subject. If you follow even a little of the advice given in it, be ready for it to turn your world upside down. The author, Rosaria Butterfield, has dedicated her life to the principle of radically ordinary hospitality and shares the observation that those who live out this principle grow in love to see strangers as neighbors and neighbors as the family of God. She says,

> They recoil at reducing a person to a category or a label—liberal, conservative, democratic, republican, gay, straight, and they see God's image reflected in the eyes of every human being on earth. Those who live out radically ordinary hospitality see their homes not as theirs at all but as God's gift to use for the furtherance of his kingdom. They open doors, they seek out the underprivileged, they know the gospel comes with a house key.[5]

### Accepting Your Limits

The invitation to community is not meant to make us feel overwhelmed and unable to measure up. Especially in an age where "friend" is defined as the hundreds of people we are connected to on social media, it is important to remember our God-given limitations.

Jesus's life modeled healthy relationship circles, from the three he was closest to—Peter, James, and John—to the twelve apostles (Matt. 10:1), to the seventy-two sent out on mission (Luke 10:1), and then to the crowds he taught and healed. British anthropologist and evolutionary psychologist Robin Dunbar created a theory that looks very similar to the Jesus model. According to Dunbar, the tightest circle the human brain is capable of connecting well with has just five people: your closest friends or family. That's followed by successive layers of fifteen (good friends), fifty (friends), one hundred and fifty (meaningful contacts), five hundred (acquaintances), and one thousand five hundred (people you can recognize).[6]

You cannot be everything to everyone. Let yourself off that hook and focus on developing deep, meaningful, transparent relationships with a few. Then make yourself open and interruptible enough to see how God can use you to disciple the people he brings into your levels of influence.

### Individual Practice

Pray for each member of your group by name each week.

Over the next two weeks, practice hospitality to build community in a new way. Don't think you have to do it the same way or at the same level as someone else in your group. Simply pray about how you can take a deeper step to be intentionally welcoming to strangers and friends.

Ideas include:

- Invite someone who needs a connection to your home for a meal or to go fishing or cycling, or to a movie or concert, or to anything else you can enjoy together.
- Fire up the grill and/or firepit and invite some friends over, being intentional about taking the conversations a little deeper than normal and consider making it a monthly gathering.
- Sign up to help on the greeting team at your church.
- Make a point to show kindness to everyone you see, whether it's engaging them in conversation at the grocery store or simply saying hello and smiling as you pass.
- Look for the outsiders in various settings and take a few extra moments to engage them.

**Leaders:** Plan a time during these two weeks to just hang out as a group and enjoy being together.

### In Community

*Group Prayer Prompts*

**Week One:** Check in with each other and give any life updates or personal prayer requests. Have someone pray for this group in particular. Pray that the Holy Spirit will guide the group into becoming closer as a community of God and that this will help each member grow in disciple-making.

**Week Two:** Check in with each other and share any life updates or personal prayer requests. Share ways that God is forming community in your lives, either in this group or in other circles. Have each person write down the name of someone they know who is not seeking God. Pray over each of these names together.

*Group Discussion*

**Week One**

1. What stood out to you in the chapter and/or the Scripture readings?
2. What role has community played in your life with Jesus over the years? How have you helped others connect with God, and how have they helped you?
3. Do you have connections outside of friends who already know Christ? Share about these, and if you do not have them this season, what steps can you take to grow those relationships?
4. What challenges to creating a deeper Christian community and/or practicing hospitality have you experienced in the past?
5. Was it hard for you to decide to commit to the type of community and commitment asked for in this group?

**Week Two**

1. How did the week one practice of community go? Share some of your experiences.
2. The church in Corinth had a high intellectual capacity but needed to work on loving and caring for each other, leading Paul to write explicitly about this issue in a letter to them. With this in mind, read 1 Corinthians 13 aloud together and discuss the following question: What gets in the way of your ability to practice the characteristics of love Paul describes? Possible answers might include busyness, exhaustion, strained relationships, unaddressed anger, sadness, or fear.
3. Spend time thinking about your relationships and sharing where you struggle. Do you have your three or so closest spiritual relationships like Peter, James, and John? Do you have your twelve with whom you enjoy table fellowship? What's the next step for you in your move toward deeper relational spirituality?
4. If you had a chance to get into the Go Deeper material, what stood out to you?

**Go Deeper**

*The Gospel Comes with a House Key: Practicing Radically Ordinary Hospitality in Our Post-Christian World*, Rosaria Butterfield

Practicing the Way: Community

"Black History Month: A Holistic and Historical Look into Community Building, Church Planting, and Coffee," interview with author and entrepreneur John Onwuchekwa, *Be the Bridge Podcast with Latasha Morrison*, episode 261

For direct links, visit pvcc.org/resources.

# Practice Two

## PRAYER

PRAYER IS LIKELY THE MOST commonly practiced of all the disciplines. We have our prayer rooms, prayer warriors, prayer teams, and prayer requests, to the point that anyone who has been close to church culture, even for a minute, is familiar with the general concept. Sharing our concerns and requests in prayer both with God and others is fairly common; but ask for much more than those traditional formats, and it starts to get a little uncomfortable.

So let's get uncomfortable together.

**Read and Meditate on**
Isaiah 6:1–8; Matthew 5 and 6; Luke 5:16, 6:12, 9:18–20, and 23–29; and Romans 8:26

A deeply transformative prayer life is not just for the quiet, contemplative monks among us. Jesus began with a rough crowd of uneducated fishermen, societal outcasts, and political zealots. He taught them to seek God in the quiet whether that was their natural personality bent or not.

> The first and most basic thing we can and must do is to keep God before our minds.
>
> **—Dallas Willard,** *The Great Omission*[1]

A life of prayer is a life of relationship with the Creator of the universe, and it is a life that is growing in the power and fruit of the Holy Spirit. It is shaped in the quiet, but it is anything but boring. Moments spent in prayer can bend reality. They can chase away the nagging doubt, fear, and anxiety that many of us carry as we, in communion with God our Father, hear him reassure us of his presence, his will, his power, and most of all, his deep love for us.

### Why Pray?

In Matthew 5, we find Jesus on a hillside overlooking the sea of Galilee. It is early in his ministry, but his popularity is spreading, and the crowds are growing. He opens what becomes the most famous sermon of all time by simply offering a series of blessings to his listeners, meeting them where they are and encouraging them (vv. 3–12). He sees them in their mourning, meekness, and the many vulnerabilities resulting from their stations in life and reassures them that they are blessed because a new kingdom is being ushered in.

He also sees through what the other rabbis and the world around them would have seen. He sees their hearts and their desire for him. He calls out their hunger for righteousness and their purity of heart and then begins to dig deeper. He calls them to a much higher way to live than they have heard before. He recounts the laws they have heard all their lives as Jews, then raises the bar. Verses thirteen to forty-eight paint a picture of the kind of life that a disciple of Jesus will live. He challenges them to live into a kingdom kind of love, honoring relationships and each other in deeper and more life-changing ways than they have ever heard before.

He doesn't just leave them with this call and ask them to keep trying harder to improve. In Matthew 6, he tells them how to do it:

- Give to the poor (1–4).
- Pray and fast with a spirit of humility (5–18).
- Trust God more than your wealth or abilities (19–34).

Giving, praying, fasting, and trusting God are all habits we can participate in and heart postures we can grow into. With grace and love, Jesus meets us where we are in every season of our lives by giving us simple tools to turn our hearts toward him. Practicing his way over time forms us from the inside out.

We will examine fasting and giving soon, but for now, let's consider how the discipline of prayer creates a space to encounter God's presence in our lives and invites the power of the Holy Spirit to work in our hearts.

---

Prayer is *all the ways in which we communicate and commune with God.*

**—Ruth Haley Barton,** *Sacred Rhythms*—emphasis original[2]

---

Time in prayer is essential to knowing the heart of God. The purpose is not to check it off our spiritual to-do list, to keep bad things from happening, or to ensure blessings come our way. The purpose isn't even to get what we ask for, though God cares deeply about you and what is on your heart. The primary purpose of prayer is God himself: experiencing his presence, enjoying his company and his love, and simply living in a relationship with him. It's not as much about what we say as it is about simply being with God.

So what are we listening for, and how do we know that what we hear, feel, or experience is from God? There is no simple answer to this question, but perhaps when we let go of the desire to understand exactly how the Spirit works and when and where the Spirit shows up, our minds will be freer to recognize God's presence all around us.

## Teach Us to Pray

In Luke 11, the disciples come to Jesus and ask him to teach them to pray. At that time, it was common for a disciple to receive prayers from their rabbi, and Jesus's disciples were no different. Often in the Gospels, Jesus's answer is less than direct when he is asked a direct question. He may use a parable or story to convey a point or refer to a prophecy from the Old Testament. But not here. His followers ask a very specific question, and he gives them a direct and practical answer, which is not a parable but a liturgy. He shares a prewritten prayer that most likely he prayed himself. And that prayer, the Lord's Prayer, has become famous worldwide and throughout history.

This important teaching of Jesus was also recorded in Matthew 6 when he shared it with the crowd on the hillside. Pause briefly to imagine Jesus teaching this prayer to his disciples, slowly reciting each phrase. Pray the words along with him in your imagination. Pause to let the Spirit fill in the gaps and transform this ancient prayer into your heart's desire for your place and time.

This, then, is how you should pray:
"Our Father in heaven, hallowed be your name,
your kingdom come, your will be done, on earth as it is in heaven.
Give us today our daily bread.
And forgive us our debts, as we also have forgiven our debtors.
And lead us not into temptation, but deliver us from the evil one."
(Matt. 6:9–13)

This prayer is full of what Jesus knows we need to say to God daily as we grow as disciples: God's sovereignty, our contentment, trust for daily provision, kingdom mindset, request for forgiveness, and protection from Satan. It is a practical prayer dealing with daily life. These themes are at the heart of what it means to follow Jesus. Jesus knows that living the life he is calling us to will not be easy, that the attributes he calls us to run completely counter to our sinful human nature. And that is why he teaches us to pray about them.

## Prayers of a King

After the Lord's Prayer, the book of Psalms is one of the best places in Scripture to learn how to pray. Psalms are songs and poems from the hearts of people who sought God in all of life's circumstances, experiencing all manner of fears, hopes, dreams, and emotions. The authors are honest about the difficulty of life and their relationship with God.

Many Psalms are attributed to King David, who was called "a man after God's own heart" (1 Sam. 13:14; Acts 13:22). This is the same man who committed murder, adultery, and rape (see 2 Sam. 11). Considering all the brokenness and failure of his own life, why was he given this highest praise? Could it be that his heart was transformed and his life changed through his prayer life?

The Psalms are an honest, raw, and lengthy prayer journal for all generations to see what is in the human heart and how God transforms us. The psalmists lamented, cried out, confessed, praised, and most of all, never stopped running toward God.

When your prayer life feels strained or stagnant, turn to the book of Psalms. Begin praying these ancient words daily and let them reveal new parts of your heart and of God's.

## Practicing Prayer

For centuries, followers of Jesus have been inspired to find new ways to reach out and connect with the Father. The practices below are rich in church history and practice, but they are not, by any means, a complete list. They are simply invitations for you to experience with God and in community with your group. Feel free to share and try others that have been meaningful to you or other members in your group during your time together.

### *Breath Prayer*

Breath prayer is a practice that has been used for hundreds of years to help clear and center the mind of Jesus's followers during times of silent meditation. It has a way of grounding you in a spiritual reality that is deeper than what is going on around you. It is the prayer of the beggar, knowing that without God you can do nothing, and it carries with it the intimacy of simply asking for what you need.

This is my go-to centering practice. As a mom of four, an extrovert, an eight on the enneagram, and a communications professional, my life and personality are nowhere near what you would call naturally contemplative. But breath prayer can stop it all in a moment. Whether in the car, still in bed in the morning, stepping outside during a chaotic afternoon at home, or even during a busy workday, breath prayer brings me back to where I need to be with

God. It reminds me that God is God and I am not. These prayers remind me of his love, that his presence is my deepest need, and that he has words of wisdom and comfort to give me in every situation.

There are many ways to go about praying through breath prayer, but in short, as you breathe in and out, repeat a true phrase about God or your desire for him. Try a rhythm of setting a five-minute timer and holding each breath for about four seconds. Breathe in during the first part of the prayer and out during the second part. Some examples include:

- "God is in control, God is always good."
- "Rabbi, I want to see."
- "Speak, Lord, your servant is listening."
- "I believe, help my unbelief."
- "I surrender all, King Jesus."
- "Open my eyes, Holy Spirit."
- "Create in me, a clean heart, oh God."
- "Let all I do, be done in love."

A wonderful example of a breath prayer from Galatians 5:22–23 was written by Sheridan Voysey and takes each attribute of love and its counter in our life to create the following prayers.

> Lord God, fill me with your Holy Spirit . . .
> I receive your love, and release my insecurity.
> I receive your joy, and release my unhappiness.
> I receive your peace, and release my anxiety.
> I receive your patience, and release my impulsiveness.
> I receive your kindness, and release my indifference.
> I receive your goodness, and release my ungodliness.
> I receive your faithfulness, and release my disloyalty.
> I receive your gentleness, and release my severity.
> I receive your self-control, and release my self-indulgence.[3]

Different phrases will be more meaningful to you at different times in your life and even during each week. Find what resonates with your heart and makes you feel most connected to God.

### *Praying the Hours*

Praying the hours, or fixed-hour prayer, is another ancient worldwide practice. It involves praying the same thing simultaneously with other believers. Although today it is often practiced in monasteries and by clergy, in the early church it was part of every believer's daily life, shaping their days around Scripture and prayer.

A typical schedule for fixed-hour prayer follows a pattern of prayers at 6 a.m., 9 a.m., noon, 3 p.m., and 6 p.m. Simpler adaptations involve a morning prayer, a midday prayer, and an evening prayer. The fixed-hour prayer is not simply stopping to pray any prayer throughout the day but includes prayers that follow a liturgy or a structured way of praying. This includes set prayers, Scripture reading, and a song or hymn. For resources and tools to practice fixed-hour prayer, see the Go Deeper section at the end of the chapter.

### *Intercessory Prayer*

In its simplest form, intercessory prayer just means praying for someone else. It is practiced in churches, small groups, and quiet places all over the Christian world. It has become so normalized that sometimes we can forget what we are actually doing. "I'm praying for you" or #prayfor(fill in the blank) has become such a quick and common response that we often offer it and move on, intending to pray but sometimes not ever getting around to it.

Technology, social media, and the 24-hour news cycle has to have created a world where we are completely overwhelmed with the needs around us. It is crippling to try to process and respond to everything, but as Christians, we cannot become numb to the power we tap into through intercessory prayer. We pray in the name of the one who drives out demons and raises the dead. We live in the power and promises of Jesus and must remember that we are praying in his authority. Our prayers have the power to move heaven, to fight spiritual battles, and to change the face of eternity. We cannot carry all the burdens of the world, but we must take seriously the call to go to battle for the people and the situations God puts specifically on our hearts.

In Isaiah 6, we find the Israelites in a period of moral and spiritual decline. They are turning away from God, and he is grieved heavily by it. God invites the prophet Isaiah into this pain and shares the burden of these lost people with him. Isaiah does not turn away from the brokenness all around him. His response to the call is, "Here am I. Send me!" (6:8).

When we partner with God to pray in his will for this world, we are echoing the response of Isaiah. We are helping to bring heaven to earth. We are not simply checking off a spiritual to-do list, but we are sharing the burden of a broken world and laying it at the feet of God. It will feel heavy and painful at times to shoulder the weight of sin and pain we see around us. Sometimes we will not even be able to articulate the words we need. The apostle Paul tells us in Romans 8:26–27 that the Holy Spirit intercedes for us in our weakness with wordless groans, searching our hearts to intercede for us within the will of God. We don't have to have the right words. We only have to show up.

There are many ways to practice this discipline, and trying something new is often helpful for personal spiritual growth. Try keeping a prayer journal of requests or prayer cards on a ring that you can bring out when you are sitting in traffic, waiting in a line, or tempted to pass a few minutes by scrolling through social media or checking the news.

"Praying the room" is an intercessory prayer practice that involves simply sitting in silence and waiting for the Spirit to bring someone to mind and guide you in praying for that person. This can be especially meaningful after a time of solitude or fasting as your mind and body are fully prepared and focused. Take the time needed to slow your mind and ask God to bring someone to you, then ask in what way they need your intercession. Wait and listen to the nudges in your heart. In these moments, trust that God is bringing prayers to your mind, and let the Spirit guide you in what to pray.

Intercessory prayer can also be applied to small groups. Consider asking each person in your group to say a prayer of encouragement over the person next to them (provide specific prompts if your group is new to praying aloud together). Groups should also practice sharing prayer requests throughout the week, encouraging each other to be vulnerable and transparent.

When prayers are answered individually and in groups, share the stories! Never hesitate to celebrate what God has done, and use these moments, both big and seemingly small, to build your faith and the faith of those around you.

> When you begin to live with joy and celebrate the things God has done, you find faith for the things he hasn't done yet.
>
> —**Pete Greig,** "For the Sake of Others"[4]

*Prayer of Examen*

The prayer of examen has been used by believers since 1522, when St. Ignatius instituted it as a way to help develop discipline, ask for God's grace, and increase our awareness of how God works daily through us and among us. Praying this way helps us grow in gratitude for how God is working in the world and our lives.

It also helps us get to know God better by training our minds to recognize his presence throughout the day.

It is traditionally used at the end of the day and involves five basic steps:

1. **Prepare:** Find a comfortable position. Quiet your mind through deep breathing. Share with God your intent in praying this way—to grow closer to him.
2. **Thanksgiving:** Thank God for the blessings of the day.
3. **Review:** Ask the Holy Spirit to help you see your day. Now, walk through your day as though you are playing a movie in your mind. What stands out? Any particular emotions or moments? Any consolations—when you felt close to God or noticed him working? Or desolations—times when you felt far from God and from who you are called to be?
4. **Respond:** Talk with God about what stood out from your day. What might God be telling you through your experiences and feelings? Take time to confess and ask forgiveness for the times you weren't at your best. Whatever comes to mind, talk with God about it.
5. **Look to tomorrow:** What are you excited about? What are you nervous about? Visualize yourself walking through the day with God and ask for his help. Spend a few more moments with God, listening to him and finding peace in his presence.

A simple form of examen can be asking yourself the following questions, or even just a few different ones each time:

- When did I feel most grateful today?
- When did I feel most alive today?
- Where did I notice God the most today?
- Are there words or actions I need to confess or forgive?

Sit with these questions awhile in search of the most authentic responses. When these questions become part of your daily rhythm, you will begin to notice that you anticipate them during the day, becoming more and more aware of God's presence in your life.

**Read and Meditate on**
1 Thessalonians 5:16–18

*Praying through Activity*

Praying while we walk, run, paint, build, and create is a meaningful way to invite God into what we are doing with our bodies and connect to him. It is a way to pray without ceasing. While walking or running around your neighborhood, simply pray for what the Holy Spirit brings to mind, partnering with God in the work he is already doing. Try question prompts like . . .

- Lord, what is your will for the people in this place?
- Who are you moving here right now?
- What are the barriers to your work here?

If praying while working on some task, let your activity keep your body busy while your mind is free to connect with God. Begin with a few moments of centering silence or breath prayer, focusing on the specific work of your hands. Let the Holy Spirit bring things to your attention to pray for in your life or the lives of others while you use the gifts and interests God has blessed you with.

Praying through activity simply requires the intentionality of pointing our minds and hearts toward God and his will in the ordinary moments of our day. Brother Lawrence has been remembered from the 1600s for the intimacy he expressed concerning his relationship to God as recorded in the book *The Practice of the Presence of God.* He advised ordinary Christians during daily activities to "lift your heart up to Him, because even the least little remembrance will please Him. You don't have to pray out loud; He's nearer than you can imagine."[5]

*Prayer Journaling and Sketching*

As you sit with God in the quiet, try opening up a blank page and grabbing something you enjoy writing with—a favorite pen, marker, or colored pencil. In the center, write a name for God, the name of someone you're praying for, or a verse or song about God that comes to mind.

Draw a shape around the words to start the doodle. This is your prayer space. Start to doodle around it, releasing your words to God in prayer. Doodle in silence or talk to God if you feel led. Add other people, names for God, or other parts of the Scripture verse to your paper. Draw a shape around each set of new words to create a separate prayer space. Doodle around these and pray. Pause and say "amen" or "Lord, hear my prayer" between each prayer space you add.

## What about Our Requests?

Jesus makes some pretty audacious claims about prayer: "Your Father who sees in secret will reward you [when you pray in secret]" (Matt. 6:6 ESV); "Ask and it will be given to you, seek and you will find, knock and the door will be opened . . ." (Matt. 7:7–11); and "If two of you on earth agree about anything they ask for, it will be done for them by my Father in heaven" (Matt. 18:19), for example.

So what happens when our life experiences with prayer don't match up to these claims, when it feels like our prayers go unanswered? Countless books have been written exploring this subject much better than I can tackle here. A place to start is simply just admitting that we don't know everything about how prayer works. We certainly don't have a special formula figured out to get all our prayers answered. Our posture is much more like a child who does not always understand why their parents answer a request in the way they do.

When it seems our prayers have gone unanswered, we should recognize that other forces are at work and consider questions like . . .

- Are we praying in God's will or our own?
- Are we asking God to alter the laws of nature or infringe on someone else's free will?
- Are other spiritual forces at work battling against the good we are praying for?

Prayer *does* change things. It bends reality and can change the face of eternity. But we must always remember that prayer is a means to an end, not the end in itself. The goal is to grow closer to God—to experience him, connect with him, and partner with him in the renewing of the world, in his kingdom coming to earth as it is in heaven. We have to submit to his will and humbly live in the reality that we will not understand "how it all works" this side of heaven.

**Individual Practice**

Remember:

> There is no bad way to pray. . . . All the great spiritual masters offer only one non-negotiable rule: you have to show up for prayer, and you have to show up regularly.
>
> —**Ronald Rolheiser,** *Prayer: Our Deepest Longing*[6]

Give each one of these prayer practices a chance this week and next. If one is especially difficult, try it a second time. If one is especially meaningful, repeat it as well. Consider incorporating one or more of these practices into your daily or weekly rhythm.

Take a walk or drive around your neighborhood, praying for neighbors you know and those you don't to move closer to Christ.

Pray for each member of your group by name.

**In Community**

*Group Prayer Prompts*

**Week One:** Set a five-minute timer and choose a breath prayer to pray silently as a group. Breathe very slowly—in for four seconds, hold for four seconds, then out for four seconds.

**Week Two:** To begin your time together, everyone prays a simple blessing (one to two sentences) over the person to their right, going in turn until everyone has been prayed for. To end, pray again for the names of people you know who are far from God.

*Group Discussion*

**Week One**

1. What stood out to you in the Scriptures?
2. What has been your relationship to prayer in the past?

3. What did God reveal to you and how did he choose to reveal it?
4. Do you have a prayer habit in this season of life? If so, what is it like?

**Week Two**

1. How did the week one practice of prayer go? Share some of your experiences.
2. When have you felt close to God in prayer?
3. Which of these practices are familiar to you? Which are new?
4. If you had a chance to get into the Go Deeper material, what stood out to you?

## Go Deeper

Practicing the Way - Prayer (practicingtheway.org/prayer): Includes a four-week lesson series that includes the topics of *Talking to God, Talking with God, Listening to God,* and *Being with God.* The site includes podcasts and a downloadable prayer companion.

*The Divine Hours*, Pocket Edition, Phyllis Tickle

Smartphone apps:

- The Common Prayer: a prayer, song, and Scripture for each day
- My Daily Office: daily prayers and Bible readings
- Hallow: daily prayer of examen
- Pray as You Go: daily prayers and meditations
- Reimagining the Examen: prayer prompts and reflections for evening prayer
- Pause: a simple way to connect with God during the day

For direct links, visit www.pvcc.org/resources.

## Practice Three

# SCRIPTURE

NOW THAT WE ARE SEVERAL weeks into this, I have a confession: I hate memorizing Scripture. I know that I need to write it on my heart (Heb. 8:10) and that it is living and active (Heb. 4:12), but memorization gives me anxiety. I've never been good at it. I know I shouldn't forget it altogether, and Scripture memorization can be an incredibly valuable practice. If you resonate with my hesitation for this practice, I have some good news for you.

The invitation to this discipline is not about what I can do with the Word of God but about what it can do in me. There is something so special and powerful about how the Holy Spirit uses the Word of God. Time and time again, when I am at a loss for what to do in a hard situation or need to be convicted of a sin in my heart, the Holy Spirit brings pieces of Scripture to my mind that I have not ever intentionally memorized. The Spirit has written it on my heart. The power in God's Word lies not in what I can do with Scripture, but what it will do in me.

## Our Remarkable Bible

The words of God are powerful. They created the world and continue to apply to human beings' daily lives across cultures and generations through the written Bible.

The Bible has been translated into more than 720 languages and is the most widely distributed work ever written, with billions of copies sold. In addition to printed copies, the YouVersion Bible app has been translated into over 800 languages and downloaded over two hundred million times.

Even from a secular standpoint, the Bible is remarkable. It has greatly influenced Western civilization, laying the groundwork for democratic forms of government and law and shaping societal values. It has also served as a fundamental source for nearly every genre of art and literature. The greatest artists—Raphael, Leonardo da Vinci, Michelangelo, Rembrandt, and others—are most remembered and appreciated for their biblical masterpieces.

We can study the Bible like a textbook, history book, poetry compilation, sociological study, self-help reference, and more. And no matter how long we study it, it will never leave us wanting for intellectual pursuits. Reading it for any purpose is beneficial as we learn about God's heart expressed throughout human history. But has it changed *your* heart?

Are you reading the Bible as a newsletter or a love letter? A textbook or storybook? When you pick up your Bible, is it mainly for information or transformation? To be transformed by Scripture, we have to go beyond using it, at best for knowledge and rules and, at worst, to prove a point or to find a loophole. To experience its changing power over our lives, we have to engage with Scripture as the true, life-giving, active words of God.

> The *study* of Scripture is important, but if we stop there, we will eventually hit a wall. Information gathering may be exhilarating and even useful at times, but in the end, our soul knows that there must be something more.
>
> **—Ruth Haley Barton,** *Sacred Rhythms*[1]

The goal of informational reading is to cover as much ground as possible to get the knowledge we need, just like we would with a self-help book, article, or social media feed. But transformational reading is about quality, not quantity. We must slow down and sit in the text. We must wait, trusting the Holy Spirit to reveal what Scripture is trying to tell us now.

**Read and Meditate on**
Psalm 19:7–11; Psalm 119:89–109;
Colossians 3:16–17; John 6:60–68; John 8:31–32

In John 8, Jesus had the Pharisees on their toes. He rebuked them for how they treated a woman caught in adultery, he confused them, along with the Jewish crowds, by his words about being the light and going where they cannot go, and then he turned to those the text says "had believed him" and tells them that if they hold to his teachings, then they truly are his disciples (8:31). Some versions say "hold to" and some say "abide" or "remain in" his word, but the meaning is the same. Jesus is saying that a marker of discipleship is how connected his followers are to his words, how much they value them, and how much time they spend with them. Disciples have a unique and intentional relationship with Scripture.

## Biblical Authority

It is an ever-increasing challenge in our culture, even in churches, to believe that the Bible is what Jesus says it is. Some reasons for this include the misuse of Scripture, the various opinions on what Scripture says about cultural issues, and the overall lack of agreement that absolute truth is even something we can find. In a "you do you," "my truth," and "fake news" world, it becomes harder and harder to trust that the Bible was authored in love by God and that it has our best interests at heart. It is harder than ever to believe that we can trust our lives to its teachings.

If you find yourself in a place of doubt regarding the authority of the Bible, take a step back and prayerfully look at it with fresh eyes. Try a time of not making it fit into every box you've been told it fits into or assumed it would fit into. Approach it simply as God's story to mankind about himself. Read it as just one of the ways he reveals who he is to you and what he wants for your life.

Try reengaging by reading through the stories of Jesus in the Gospels or a section of the Psalms or whole, shorter books like Micah or James. Try reading the larger chunks in a long, relaxed setting, letting the full context settle on your heart. Give the Holy Spirit time to convict your heart that it is true and worth submitting your will to.

There are lots of resources that help answer some of the bigger questions about biblical authority and how the Bible stands up to its critics. See the Go Deeper section for a few to start with. Above all, don't give up on it. Transformation happens when disciples relate to the Scriptures in love and submit to Jesus's words and life.

## In Context

As you grow in your relationship with Scripture, context is crucial. The most obvious way to look at this is by considering the historical context of the actual text itself. Who is the audience, where and when was the text written, and how was it originally received, understood, and applied? This information is readily available in most Bibles or through a quick Google search and worth repeated looks as you dive deeper into Scripture. This deeper level of engagement with the text can help you relate to it in new ways to be challenged and changed by your reading.

Another deeply formative way of relating to Scripture is to pay attention to the modern cultural context. The words of God are for all people for all times, so it's important to pay attention to the idea that anything we glean from them must be as true for a businessman in New York as it is for a child in remote Africa, a priest in Italy, or a stay-at-home mom in Alabama. You get the point.

A powerful example of this is the slave-owners' Bible. In many known contexts, slave owners focused on verses that suited their needs, such as, "Slaves, submit to your masters" (1 Pet. 2:18). The slave-owners' Bible, however, took this to a new level. It was created in the early 1800s by British missionaries to the West Indies for the purpose of converting and educating slaves without giving them any ideas that might incite rebellion or liberation. According to Anthony Schmidt, associate curator of Bible and Religion in America at the Museum of the Bible in Washington, DC, the slave owner's Bible cuts about 90 percent of the Old Testament and 50 percent of the New Testament.[2] When you consider the amount of the Bible that sides with the weak and vulnerable, it is no surprise that most of the Bible would have to be eliminated to support their narrative.

Without considering context, both ancient and modern, we will inevitably default to our own limited understanding and biases. In doing this, we risk being misinformed and hurtful to others. When we create a gospel that is only good news for us, in our culture, and with our resources, education, and sin struggles, we have robbed the text of its transforming power over our lives.

### Tools for Engagement

There are many time-tested ways to follow Jesus and be transformed by Scripture. A few are outlined in the following sections. As you try these practices and others, seek the wisdom of the Holy Spirit in incorporating one or many into your daily life.

*Lectio Divina—Divine or Sacred Reading*

Lectio Divina (lex-ee-oh day-vee-nah) is an approach that prepares us to listen for the Word of God spoken to us at the present moment. This can be done alone or in community. As a group, it can really bring you together as you see the Holy Spirit working in each group member's heart in a different way.

- Begin in silence, aware of God's presence with you and listening for the Spirit.
- **Read:** Take a short passage (six to eight verses) and listen for the word or phrase addressed to you. Read it slowly, pausing often, until a word or phrase pops out. You may even try reading it out loud. Then repeat it to yourself, pause, and savor it as a word just for you. Allow it to deepen in your heart.
- **Reflect:** Read the passage again, listening for how it connects with your life. Ask, what in my life needs to hear this word or phrase? Where am I in this scene? What do I hear? How does this story connect to my life? This doesn't have to be a major revelation; let God lead you in discovering a word for the moment.

- **Respond:** What is my response to God based on what I read? What is God inviting me into? Read again, listening for your own deepest and truest response. Share your response with God in prayer or in a journal. Keep it honest, simple, and heartfelt. God wants to hear from you.
- **Rest:** Read again, releasing and resting in God as a parent, yielding everything to him in love.
- **Resolve:** Live it out. Meditate on the passage or the word or phrase and listen to go deeper throughout the day. Trust God to work in your life and transform your heart as you submit to him.

*Questions Jesus Asks*

The Gospels record over eighty questions between Jesus and the people he encountered. This practice involves reading a Gospel and stopping anytime Jesus asks someone a question. Pause and imagine Jesus is asking you the same question.

For example, in John 1:35–38 (ESV) we read,

> The next day again John was standing with two of his disciples, and he looked at Jesus as he walked by and said, "Behold, the Lamb of God!" The two disciples heard him say this, and they followed Jesus. Jesus turned and saw them following and said to them, "What are you seeking?"

At this point in the text, stop and ask yourself, "What am I seeking?" What are you seeking right now? What are you hoping Jesus will do for you? Talk to God about the question and your answer.

*Placing Yourself in the Story*

This practice slows us down and allows our imagination to help the Scripture come alive. It helps us tap deeper into God's creative nature within us. It works best with stories and parables, picturing every detail about the setting, characters, and what God is trying to share with the original audience and with you in this time and place.

For an example, use Luke 10:38–42 or John 9. Read one of these passages. Imagine the environment. What does it look like? What does it smell like? What do you physically feel? What do you see and hear? Can you taste anything? Enter the scene. Choose to be an observer or select one of the characters and try to become that person. What are you feeling? What are you thinking? What would you like to say? Interact with one of the characters in the story in your imagination. Ask him or her questions and imagine their answers. Talk to God about your experience.

*Dialogue with God*

In our busy lives, it is much too easy to read over Scripture and then move on quickly to the next task. Remembering that the Bible is how God speaks to us helps us utilize Scripture to converse with him.

As you read any portion of Scripture, try picturing Jesus in the room with you. What is he wearing? What expression is on his face? Can you imagine the touch of his hand on yours? Tell him how you feel about the passage. Ask him questions and wait to hear an answer. Talk with him about how it applies to your life (or how you feel it doesn't apply) and the challenges it brings. And finally, ask for guidance to let the Scripture transform you to be more like Jesus.

*Memorizing Scripture*

This practice is probably the most familiar and may even be the most dreaded by some (including myself). Jesus and his followers lived in a time of oral tradition, where Scripture memorization was vital to knowing the heart and will of God. With most of us carrying hundreds of Bible translations around in our pockets, this practice can become somewhat lost.

Try to memorize a small section of Scripture over the next few weeks as a group. As you plant it in your heart, pray about applying it as well.

**Tips:** Start small, say it out loud, write it, draw it, listen to it, use flashcards and sticky notes, work with a partner or small group, use an online tool or app, and even translate it into another language if you are bilingual.
Example verses to begin with: **Psalm 23, Ephesians 3:16–19, Philippians 4:6–7,** or **Colossians 3:12–17.**

*Discovery Bible Study*

The Discovery Bible Study Method (at discoverybiblestudy.org) is a simple and powerful way not only to engage more deeply with Scripture as an individual but also to deepen engagement in a group setting or with a nonbeliever or nominal Christian. The method is centered around asking four simple questions of the text.

- **Question 1:** What does this story tell me about God?
  This question pulls out why we come to the Bible in the first place. The point of Scripture is to point us to God and show us what he is like. This may not be obvious at first, but as you dig deeper and listen to the Spirit, you'll find that God's character is deeply stamped in every passage.

- **Question 2:** What does this story tell me about people? This question holds up a mirror to who we are and why we need God. For many, this question becomes intensely personal. What does this story reveal about myself? It shows us all the ways in which we fall—but often, it also shows all the ways that God pulls us back up again.

- **Question 3:** If this is really God's Word, what changes would I have to make in my life?
This is where Discovery Bible Study departs most from traditional Bible study. Often we come to the Bible to learn about God. This question moves us toward transformation. When we identify what the Spirit is telling us through the Word, we then have to wrestle with how to put it into practice.

- **Question 4:** Who am I going to tell?
This final question leans into the point of spiritual formation for the sake of others. When we experience life change, our story becomes more powerful, as it combines the information of the Scripture with the transformation in a life right in front of you.

### Find Your Scripture Practices

As you move into the individual and group practice, take the time to really live in each of these Scripture practices. Use each tool until you understand its purpose and figure out which one increases your love of Scripture in this season of life. As with the other disciplines, this is not an exhaustive list; also share in your group other ways of engaging with Scripture that you have found meaningful.

## Individual Practice

Try each of these practices during the next two weeks. If one feels awkward or taxing, try it again before moving on.

Pray for each member of your group by name each week.

## In Community

*Group Prayer Prompts*

**Week One:** Pray the Lord's Prayer from Matthew 6:9–13. Go around the circle with each group member praying a section slowly out loud.

> Our Father in heaven, hallowed be your name,
> your kingdom come, your will be done,
> on earth as it is in heaven.
> Give us today our daily bread.
> And forgive us our debts, as we also have forgiven our debtors.
> And lead us not into temptation, but deliver us from the evil one.

**Week Two:** Begin by having someone pray a Psalm for the group. Choose your own or use Psalm 63:1–5 or 92:1–8. End with one person praying the Great Commission from Matthew 28:19–20 aloud, then pausing to let each member insert their name after "go" and the name of their neighborhood in the place of "the world." Example: "Therefore go (Courtney) and make disciples of all (Lakewood), baptizing them in the name of the Father and of the Son and of the Holy Spirit, and teaching them to obey everything I have commanded you. And surely I am with you always, to the very end of the age."

*Group Discussion*

**Week One**

1. What stood out to you in the chapter and/or the Scripture readings?
2. What is your general view of Scripture? Do you trust it? Do you use it as an active template to shape your life with God?
3. What have been your expectations of Scripture in the past? Do we ever place expectations on Scripture that it was never meant to fulfill?
4. How does your view of Scripture compare to how you view Jesus?
5. Practice one of the ways mentioned in this chapter to engage Scripture together.

**Week Two**

1. How did the week one practice of engaging with Scripture go? Share some of your experiences.
2. How have you engaged Scripture in the past?
3. Which practice resonated with you the most this week, and would you share a word you heard, big or small, from the Lord?
4. Practice one of the ways mentioned in the chapter to engage Scripture together.
5. If you had a chance to get into the Go Deeper in memorization, what did you memorize? Was it difficult?

### Go Deeper: Same Bible, Different Perspectives

If you have been a longtime follower of Jesus, it is sometimes helpful to read the Bible in a slightly different arrangement or with a new perspective to inspire your imagination and help you relate to Scripture in a new way. Here are a few resources to consider.

*The New Testament in Color: A Multiethnic Bible Commentary,* Esau McCaulley and others (ed.)

*The New Testament in Its World: An Introduction to the History, Literature, and Theology of the First Christians,* N. T. Wright and Michael Bird

*The Book of Psalms: A Translation with Commentary,* Robert Alter

**Other Resources**

*Savoring God's Word: Cultivating the Soul-Transforming Practice of Scripture Meditation,* Jan Johnson

*Discovering Lectio Divina: Bring Scripture into Ordinary Life,* James Wilhoit and Evan Howard

*Shaped by the Word: The Power of Scripture in Spiritual Formation,* M. Robert Mulholland Jr.

*Seven Things I Wish Christians Knew about the Bible,* Michael F. Bird

Smartphone apps:

- Lectio 365: morning and night prayer and Scripture
- Versify: Scripture memorization

Text Messages sermon series, Jonathan Storment, Pleasant Valley Church of Christ, Little Rock, AR, April–June 2024

For direct links, visit www.pvcc.org/resources.

# Practice Four

## SILENCE AND SOLITUDE

I HAVE NEVER BEEN DESCRIBED as quiet. Every report card I received in elementary school noted "talks too much" in the conduct section. And I come by it honestly. My whole side of our family likes to laugh and tell stories, and we will get louder the longer we are together. So you can assume correctly that this pair of practices, solitude and silence, did not come easily.

> **Read and Meditate on**
> Matthew 14:6–13; Mark 6:30–32; Luke 4:1–2, 14–15; Luke 5:16; Luke 6:12–13; Luke 22:39–44

Part of the beauty of these invitations from Jesus is that they truly are for everyone. Disciples don't have to pick which side of Jesus they follow based on their personality. We don't have to choose practices that fit our comfort zone or lifestyle, whether we are a quiet contemplative, an active servant, a public speaker, or a passionate justice-seeker. There is so much to be gained by everyone in the quiet.

Jesus often used silence and solitude to draw near to God and gain strength and comfort, and he taught his disciples to do the same. The Scriptures listed illustrate a distinct rhythm in Jesus's life: He engages the people around him, then retreats to be with God. I can imagine the disciples' frustration when they are looking for him to act or speak or take charge, and he retreats in prayer. Times when the crowds are seeking healing and answers that only Jesus can give, and he has stepped away. They learned by watching him retreat and also by working through the rub of his absence how much he valued and depended on time alone with God.

For me, this pair of practices has become essential to my faith. More than anything, they have helped me know God on a deeper level and allowed me to hear his voice more clearly. They are the answer when I feel worn out or bogged down. They are the answer when my faith is lacking. When I question and doubt, the Holy Spirit reminds me that I can trust God because I know him and have recognized his goodness again and again through time in silence and solitude.

I simply could not even try to be the wife, mother, friend, or minister I want to be without them. In silence and solitude, I have come to know God's faithfulness daily, as he is *always* there when I wait and listen.

### Same But Different

Silence and solitude go hand in hand, but considering them separately is helpful, as it draws out the unique benefits both practices bring. Silence is nearly impossible to achieve without solitude, but solitude doesn't have to be completely silent. That may sound too much like "a square is a rectangle, but a rectangle is not a square," but bear with me.

**Spiritual solitude** is being alone with God and God only.
**Spiritual silence** is eliminating any outside stimulation, words, music, or ideas to focus on the prompting of the Holy Spirit. It's about God's heart speaking to your heart.

Author Ruth Haley Barton has taught and practiced silence and solitude for decades. Her insight is invaluable, and I couldn't describe solitude any better than she does in her book *Sacred Rhythms*:

> Solitude . . . is a place in time that is set apart for God and God alone, a time when we unplug and withdraw from the noise of interpersonal interactions, from the noise, busyness and constant stimulation associated with life in the company of others. . . . Most important, solitude is a place inside myself where God's Spirit and my spirit dwell together in union. This place within me is private and reserved for intimacies that God and I share. . . . It is a place where I can give myself with abandon . . . knowing that I am completely safe from anyone else's curious gaze or judgmental glance.[1]

Barton says in her book *Invitation to Silence and Solitude* that we are starved for quiet. In times of solitude, when we put away the books, music, podcasts, and prayer lists, we experience the presence of God himself in the sound of sheer silence.[2]

### Alone Together

The average American's attention span in 2022 was eight seconds. Our addiction to distraction and our relentless multitasking has created a pace of daily life that makes it almost impossible to sit alone for very long, much less to sit alone in silence. But to transform our hearts to be more like Jesus, we must stop long enough and regularly enough to hear from him. Can you imagine expecting a solid marriage without being alone with your spouse? To have a real relationship with anyone, we have to take time to be alone together.

The Holy Spirit has words of wisdom, comfort, and rebuke for each of us in the situations we face today. In silence and solitude, we face our true selves, with all our brokenness, sometimes knowing what we need to confront, and other times facing our lostness in a new way. It may feel uncomfortable at first, but stick with it.

Time in silence and solitude also trains us to listen to others. James, the brother of Jesus, leans into this in James 1:19 when he advises us to be quick to listen and slow to speak. I've tried to just *be* more like that. It's never gone well or lasted long despite my best intentions. Just trying harder to control our tongues through willpower proves futile. Over time, however, practicing silence and solitude can change your heart and allow you to grow in loving and respecting those around you by how well you listen.

> In Silence, God ceases to be an object and becomes an experience.
>
> **—Thomas Merton,** New Seeds of Contemplation

**Growing in Compassion**

In 2011, the *Harvard Gazette* published a study on mindfulness involving participants who meditated an average of twenty-seven minutes per day for eight weeks. At the end of the study, pre- and post-MRI results showed an increase in gray matter density in each person's hippocampus. This area in the brain is known for memory, self-awareness, compassion (hang on to that word), and introspection.[3]

One morning recently I was volunteering to sort T-shirt orders for the PTA at our local elementary school. The vice principal came on the intercom with some announcements and then played the Pledge of Allegiance. What followed really got my attention. She invited the entire school into a moment of silence. This was not in response to anything in particular, as is done with a memorial, but it was a daily practice the school engaged in. I am sure in decades past that time would have been spent openly in prayer, but it was striking to me to see the wisdom of Jesus being leaned into in this secular setting.

In the Old Testament, God is described as compassionate more than a dozen times. From the beginning, in Exodus 34:6–7, God uses the word compassionate—or in Hebrew, *rakhum*—to describe his character. In this story, God has just freed his people from oppression in Egypt, and they are waiting for Moses to come down the mountain with a word from God. In their impatience, they decide to make idols of gold to worship instead of waiting on the God who delivered them. God is angry with their actions, but he responds to Moses with this description of his character: "The Lord, the Lord, the compassionate and gracious God, slow to anger, abounding in love and faithfulness" (Exod. 34:6).

Flip over to the New Testament, and you will see repeatedly where Jesus is "moved with compassion" for someone in need, such as in Matthew 9:35–38 and Matthew 14:13–21 KJV, just to name a couple. These have always been my favorite descriptions of what is happening in Jesus's life. This simple phrase sets a scene of deep love in action. It illustrates life-changing love that wins over any situation's pressure or problem.

Our God is compassionate. Our rabbi shows us how to live compassionately and models how to grow in compassion. Modern science also affirms that you can *physically* grow in your ability to be compassionate simply by spending just a few minutes a day in silence.

The Christian practices of silence and solitude involve mindfulness and meditation, like our school and the Harvard study are reaching for, but they are much more powerful. These practices invite the Holy Spirit to do the real work of transformation in your heart. As the renowned Dutch priest Henri Nouwen put it, "Solitude is not a private, therapeutic place (like mindfulness and meditation); rather, it is the place of conversion. There, the old self dies, and the new self is born."[4]

### But What Do We Do?

Hopefully by now you are with me in recognizing the importance of this practice duo. So you carve out the time, sit down, and what next? What do you do with your mind and body? How do you remain still and manage to quiet all the internal noise and restlessness? These questions are common, and the answers vary.

Start by remembering that all the practices are invitations from God to connect with him. Accept the invitation to turn off the noise and let go. Psalm 46:10—"Be still, and know that I am God"—was written by a group of Levites who served as musicians in the temple. "Be still" in this verse literally means "Let go of your grip." These words were written for the gathered followers of God to help them know where to start. They show us that we will have a deeper understanding of God, but first we have to let go and be still.

Silence the world around you—no music, podcasts, or books outside the Bible. Take a few deep breaths and settle in, removing as many expectations from your mind as you can. Let go of your worry, your to-dos, and your inner monologue, and just be still with God.

For me, time in silence is shorter and more frequent in my weekly rhythm than extended solitude. More often than not,

I begin my daily time with God in silence, utilizing a ten- or fifteen-minute timer and calling on the practice of breath prayer when my mind refuses to settle. I focus simply on the love God has for me and being with him alone. Some days, it's simply the time it takes me to drink my first cup of coffee in the quiet before the kids are up. I imagine enjoying that time with Jesus as if he were sitting in the room with me. Other times, it is before my feet even hit the floor, as I surrender the different activities, worries, and needs of the day at the feet of my Father and accept his grace and provision. Throughout the day, moments of waiting can turn into holy times of connection with God when, instead of reaching for the phone or radio, I pause, breathe deeply, and listen to God as I take in the world around me.

Times of silence are not the place for you to do the talking, so you can put away the prayer lists for a few moments and just be with God. The goal is not to wait for an audible divine word, although God can and does surprise those who seek him in the way he gets our attention. The goal is to train ourselves to wait and listen, not relying on our thoughts, ideas, and convictions to transform us, but letting the Holy Spirit do the heavy lifting of cultivating fruit in our lives.

Solitude is similar, but it lends itself to longer stints and leaves more room for reading Scripture and prayer. Silence should be part of your time in solitude, but don't feel that to practice solitude well you have to be completely quiet without thought or prayer for hours on end. The time you spend in solitude is about you and God, blending your voices and hearts through quiet reflection, prayer, and Scripture.

The ability to practice solitude and the logistical ease of doing so will vary in different seasons of life. Even in especially busy seasons, it is important to incorporate shorter and longer periods into your life rhythms. Short amounts of daily silence with longer stints in solitude, like several hours or even a day or more, planned into your monthly and yearly calendar will make a significant difference throughout your lifetime.

> We are driven by our inner emptiness to a self-seeking, anxious search for fullness in the next round of activities, accomplishments, or relationships. . . . For there is nothing that fills like the Love that is God. Not only does the love of God come to us in solitude, the love of God begins to pour through us to others.
>
> **—Ruth Haley Barton,** "Solitude: In God for the World"[5]

This essential pair of practices takes time to get comfortable with. Learning to quiet our minds will not feel successful at first. Our minds and bodies will likely be restless and anxious as we subconsciously or consciously push aside the deeper desires and pain that we typically ignore through our daily distractions. But this is where it gets good—as God begins to reveal things to us from our deepest places.

Jesus's brother, who no doubt watched Jesus model these practices often throughout his life, assures us in James 4:8 that when we "draw near to God, he will draw near to [us]" (ESV). The real heart work can begin in this quiet, holy place, alone and silent before God. As we practice this more and more and grow closer and closer to our Creator, we begin to see that our body and soul long for solitude, which is a longing for God, a reflection of our deepest desire.

## Hearing God's Voice

Have you ever heard a pastor share the story of the pious man in the flood? He's sitting on a rooftop, praying for help. He turns down rescue from all sides, a lifejacket, a boat, a helicopter, and he drowns. When he meets God, he is frustrated that God did not save him, to which God replies, "I sent you a lifejacket, a boat, and a helicopter."

This story is often used with a "God helps those who help themselves" message, but I see it as a reminder that there is no limit to how God speaks to us and gets our attention. It can be through others, it can be quiet or loud, it can be unexpected or fervently waited on. We can't predict how God will show up, but we can be sure that he is always there. It is up to us to quiet our lives and open our hearts and imaginations enough to hear him and recognize his voice.

It's easy to talk ourselves out of giving God the "credit" for answered prayers, blessings, and nudges. Sometimes, it seems too presumptuous to assume we know what God is up to. Other times, we are too cynical to think that God was involved in a situation. In both cases, we get stuck when we try to overthink and overanalyze.

Silence and solitude help us overcome our overthinking as we begin to recognize the gentle whisper of God, and he begins to bring things to mind that affirm his presence. They provide a place to invite Jesus into our lives—because Jesus goes where he is welcomed.

Personally, I most often experience his presence and goodness in nature and in other people. Sometimes it's in the people I love most, and other times it's an interaction with a complete stranger where it feels like a deeper understanding or knowing was shared. I have also learned to stop and seek his presence in silence and solitude when going through a difficult situation, a relational conflict, or an area of ministry in need of work. Times of need and intentional seeking like this strengthen my faith as I have begun to recognize that the Holy Spirit is always at work in my soul. These extended times of seeking God for a specific purpose have also influenced my daily prayer life, helping me gain confidence in hearing his voice and discerning his will.

Fewer and farther between are those more memorable moments when I felt a physical presence, or a stranger shared words of wisdom and encouragement with me, leaving me with no doubt that God had prompted them. These are amazing experiences, and I go back to them often when my faith weakens, but they are not the norm, at least for me.

In all these cases, both routine and extraordinary, the presence of God feels like being known, loved, and equipped for good works. It feels like the most authentic experience I can imagine in the moment. It feels like tangible goodness and truth.

If you don't yet have a story like those to draw from, take heart. God is there and is listening. Living in the tension of longing for God and discerning his presence is part of living in the now and not yet of the kingdom of God. If you are unsure about how God is speaking to you, you are not alone and not on the outside of his favor. Paul reminds us in 1 Corinthians 13:12 that "now we see only a reflection as in a mirror; then we shall see face to face." Even David, a man after God's own heart, prayed in Psalm 27:9 for God to show up, pleading for God not to hide his face.

Our distractions, doubts, and sins can separate us from the ability to hear God's voice, but God assures us that he "will never leave you nor forsake you" (Josh. 1:5) and that he will always draw near to those who draw near to him (James 4:8). Keep listening. Keep seeking him, and open yourself to new ways he may be trying to get your attention.

## Individual Practice

Pray for each member of your group by name each week.

If you are new to these practices, they will not feel successful at first. Your mind and body will likely be restless and anxious, subconsciously or consciously pushing aside the deeper feelings, longings, and pain that are typically ignored during daily distractions. But don't quit. This is where it really gets good, as God begins to reveal things from your deepest places.

- **Week One:** Set a timer and spend five minutes in silence every day, or commit your drive time to silence all week, or both. Put your phone out of reach, and turn off the radio and streaming services.

- **Week Two:** Spend thirty to sixty minutes in solitude once during the week. To help structure your time, remember there is no one way to practice solitude, and the more you experience it, the more you will feel open to letting God guide your time. But sometimes having a plan can lessen anxiety and help you make the most of your time. Try this simple formula to help get you started:

    - **Begin in silence:** Set a timer for a time of open, receptive, quiet breathing or breath prayer.
    - **Read Scripture and journal** any responses or questions. If you need a place to start, pick a Psalm or read from a Gospel.
    - Spend time in **intercessory prayer.** Sit in the quiet and wait for God to bring names and situations to your mind that need to be lifted into his presence.
    - End by **reciting and meditating on the Lord's Prayer**. Let the words of Matthew 6:9–13 flow through you as you talk to God.

### In Community

*Group Prayer Prompts*

**Week One:** Set a five-minute timer and sit in silence to begin your time together. Encourage group members to use a breath prayer to stay focused (see Practice Two).

**Week Two:** Repeat the week one prayer prompt. After you've sat in silence together, let the Holy Spirit help you look outward. Share something God has revealed to you about his goodness in this season of life or even this week. Use this time to practice sharing the difference God makes in your life as you would share it with someone who is far from God.

*Group Discussion*

**Week One**

1. What stood out to you in the chapter and/or the Scripture readings?
2. Do these practices come easy, or are they challenging?
3. Do you want to sit with God? Do you have any questions for, anger with, or resentment toward God that needs to be addressed?

**Week Two**

1. How did the week one practices of solitude and silence go? Share some of your experiences.
2. Was there any awkwardness or negativity you had to work through?
3. Was it difficult to give these practices the time needed to create meaningful heart change?
4. What adjustments can you make to prioritize times of silence and solitude in the next few weeks and months?
5. If you had a chance to get into the Go Deeper material, what stood out to you?

**Go Deeper**

"Silence and Solitude," episodes 1 and 2, *John Mark Comer Teachings* podcast, January 2022

*Sacred Rhythms,* Ruth Haley Barton, Chapter 2

*Strengthening the Soul of Your Leadership Podcast,* Invitation to Solitude and Silence, season 5, Ruth Haley Barton

*When the Soul Listens,* Jan Johnson

*Hearing God,* Dallas Willard

For direct links, visit www.pvcc.org/resources.

## Practice Five

# FASTING

I GREW UP IN A church tradition that values what is *and is not* in the Bible. I often heard older church members say publicly and privately that we "speak where the Bible speaks and we are silent where the Bible is silent," paraphrasing a quote from an 1809 declaration by Restoration Movement leader Thomas Campbell.[1]

Even though this idea often proceeded a critique of another denomination, it did create a culture that went to the Bible with all questions. The spirit was rooted in a desire to navigate life in a way that honors God and is true to his teachings. I appreciate and have been blessed by the deep respect and love of the Bible that it instilled in me. But it does leave me with some (okay, lots) of questions. One of those is: What happened to fasting?

**Read and Meditate on**

Exodus 34:28; Esther 4:16; Daniel 9:3–5; Joel 2:12; Matthew 6:16–18; Luke 4:1–2; Luke 18:11–12; Acts 13:2–3; Acts 14:23

### A Brief History

Throughout the Old and New Testaments, different types of fasts are referenced over seventy times. The first is Moses on Mount Sinai, as he goes without food and water for forty days and nights to prepare to meet with God and receive the Ten Commandments (Deut. 9:9). Then, just a few verses later, after coming down from the mountain and seeing God's people in rebellion, he fasts again for forty days and nights to petition God for his forgiveness of the people (Deut. 9:18–19).

The Bible is full of examples of the people of God seeking him through fasting, from Moses to Daniel, Elijah, Ahab, citizens of Nineveh, Paul and Barnabas, and so many more. The biblical story shows leaders, entire people groups, and individuals accepting God's invitation to fast. Their stories and lives are vastly different, but they are all seeking God. They fast as a way to encounter his presence, will, wisdom, strength, forgiveness, and protection.

Esther, Ezra, and Jehoshaphat sought God's protection through fasting (Esther 4:16; Ezra 8:21–28; 2 Chron. 20:3). Anna fasted for the coming of the redemption of Israel (Luke 2:37), and Jesus tells the disciples in Matthew 17:21 that fasting is a tool to fight demonic power.

Jesus valued fasting and used it to prepare himself to fulfill his purpose. When the time came to begin his public ministry, he first fasted forty days in the desert (Matt. 4; Luke 4). Back up just a couple of verses in Matthew's account, and we see that chapter 3 ends with Jesus's baptism.

Jesus came up from the water of baptism, and "the heavens were opened and he saw the Spirit of God descending like a dove and settling on him. And a voice from heaven said, 'This is my dearly loved Son, who brings me great joy'" (Matt. 3:16–17 NLT). What better time could there have been to launch into his first public sermon than with an introduction from God himself? But instead, the next verse tells us that Jesus was led into a time of fasting.

In the Sermon on the Mount (Matt. 5–6), giving, praying, and fasting are taught as vital practices for discipleship. All three are assumed in the life of a disciple, as Jesus begins each teaching with "*when* you give . . . *when* you pray . . . and *when* you fast. . . ."

Fasting was a regular part of Jesus's culture and his personal rule of life. It was common practice for Jews and early Christians to fast as often as twice a week, on Wednesdays and Fridays until 3 p.m. As early as 208 AD, the early church father Tertullian wrote *On Fasting*, the first Christian book addressing the practice. In the fourth century, Marcella, a Roman Christian woman, opened up her home after her husband's passing and used her wealth to invite people into the disciplines of Bible study, prayer, and fasting.

Many works and references to Christian fasting followed, including one by Augustine in the fifth century and another by Thomas Aquinas around 1265 AD. Christian leaders throughout the centuries, including Martin Luther, John Calvin, Jonathan Edwards, John Wesley, Dietrich Bonhoeffer, and C. S. Lewis, all taught and practiced fasting. It would be hard to find an early influential Christian leader who did not emphasize the importance of this discipline. Fasting was never a nominal, obscure practice for a select few. It was an integral practice in the life of everyday disciples as well as in revival movements of God within communities.

From the earliest days of the church, fasting has been recognized as an important way to draw near to God, deepen one's relationship with him, and seek His help in times of special need. Nearly all of the great spiritual leaders of the church, as well as ordinary believers who have been noted for their devotion to God, have practiced fasting.

**—Thomas A. Tarrants,** "The Place of Fasting in the Christian Life"[2]

When considering the overwhelming number of examples of fasting throughout church history, I have to ask again. . . . What happened to fasting?

If fasting was so important in the lives of the One we are following and those who first followed him, why does it seem to be one of the practices most often overlooked in our homes and churches? In his book *Celebration of Discipline*, Richard Foster cites that between 1861 and 1954, he could not find one book published on Christian fasting.[3] While fasting never completely disappeared from the teachings of leaders during this time, this public distancing from the practice is worth notice.

It does not take much imagination to figure out why the practice of fasting lost popularity. After all, who wants to talk about self-denial in a culture that preaches self-gratification and self-actualization? Even in Christian communities, we avoid and explain away disciplines like fasting and suffering. But in doing so, we cut short our ability to grow as disciples and diminish our capacity to know Christ better in and through our suffering (Phil. 3:10). As we seek to follow Jesus today, we must consider what might be missing in our spiritual formation by neglecting God's invitation to fast.

## What Fasting Is and Is Not

Fasting is not about harnessing some spiritual superpower to get what we want from God. It is not about proving how holy we are, to God or anyone else, by what we are willing to sacrifice. Instead, fasting is, as Gretchen Ronnevik writes in her book *Ragged*, "an act of stepping into the power of God, when our souls need evidence of His sufficiency. It often brings clarity or peace and is a wonderful gift to exercise when our coping skills are no longer effective."[4]

> Fasting is going without food for a set amount of time to awaken our body and soul to our deep hunger and need for God. It's one of the most powerful—and neglected—of all of Jesus's practices.
>
> **—Practicing the Way,** "The Fasting Practice"[5]

We are constantly bombarded with things to do, see, and experience, and fasting reminds us that God is enough—we don't need anything more. When Christians follow Jesus in the practice of fasting, they are saying that Jesus is enough and that they trust him with their whole lives.

In the classic literary work *Llama Llama Holiday Drama*, the main character, a cartoon llama, has a complete meltdown after living in the hustle and bustle of the winter holiday season, screaming, "Too much music, too much stuff, too much making, too much fluff!" To which his mother calmly responds, "Sometimes we should take a rest, and hold the ones we love the best."[6]

While this thought also leans into the practice of Sabbath that we will get to soon, for me fasting is a way to say with my whole body, *That's enough of the "too much" for today. I've had enough of the overindulgence and overstimulation of life, and I need a break.* And the more I practice it, the more I look forward to it as a time of respite to help me quiet my body and mind.

**Christian Fasting Is . . .**

- **Trust:** Our daily habits show that we know God has the desire and ability to meet our needs and believe he will follow through. We seek *him*, not even the food that physically sustains us, for the deepest needs in our souls.
- **Training:** As we practice "not doing," we grow in self-control, which will help us in every other part of our

lives. With each growing hunger pain, we also increase our capacity to show empathy to our brothers and sisters who regularly go without.

- **Surrender:** As we voluntarily deny ourselves something vital to our physical lives, we open our hearts to receive and rely on the power of the Holy Spirit. Each time we deny our hunger, it is a physical reminder of surrendering our lives to Jesus as King.

When I first began a regular practice of fasting, there came a time a few months in when I had gained weight, as you do when you get older, and I needed to cut back. I began thinking through what kind of diet changes I needed to make and was conflicted about what to do with my regular day of fasting. I worried that fasting while actively trying to lose weight would somehow taint my motives and negate the spiritual benefits I was seeking through fasting.

The Christian practice of fasting is different from dieting or fasting for a medical procedure. But it is still deeply physical and that is okay. Too often, we discount the importance of our physical bodies in relation to our spirituality. But from the first page of Genesis, God shows us that what we do with our bodies matters. We are not just dust. We are dust *and* Spirit (Gen. 2:7), and so what we do with our bodies—or do not do with them—is deeply spiritually formative.

Fasting is much more than a diet, but it does have some significant health benefits. These are worth noting and appreciating along with the spiritual benefits because God cares about our physical bodies.

- At twelve hours: The body starts to burn fat, the digestive system goes into sleep mode, and the body begins to heal.

- At fourteen hours: The body starts to use stored fat for energy, and human growth hormone begins to increase.
- At sixteen hours: The body begins to burn more fat.
- At eighteen hours: Human growth hormone levels increase dramatically.
- At twenty-four hours: Autophagy begins, which is a process that cleans out damaged cells and regenerates new ones. Ketones, acids that your body makes when it breaks down fat for energy, are also released into the bloodstream.

Our body can also connect us in prayer. Through fasting, we pray with our entire body. The pangs of our stomachs prompt us into prayer and reflection as we connect with God on a physical level while reaching for him intellectually and emotionally. Just like combining different learning styles when you study for an exam increases your learning potential, pointing your whole self, body, and soul toward God transforms your heart in a powerful way. Richard Foster writes, "More than any other Discipline, fasting reveals the things that control us. This is a wonderful benefit to the true disciple who longs to be transformed into the image of Jesus Christ."[7]

Let that quote sink in a minute. Are you turned off by the phrase "true disciple"? Think back to the first lesson on desire and ask yourself: Is my deepest desire really to be more like Christ? If the answer is yes, fasting can be seen not as a dreaded command to follow but as a gift. Receive it as wise advice from your brother Jesus. Foster goes on to say that we often cover up our negative desires like pride, anger, and bitterness with food. We see this as the term "hangry" has entered our shared vocabulary. We now have a word that blames a missed meal or even snack for negative behaviors like irritability and impatience. Instead of excusing, fasting leans in. It allows us to shine a light on our poor reactions and emotions and deal with them through the power of the Holy Spirit as David did in Psalm 35:13, when he wrote, "I humbled my soul with fasting" (KJV).

### How and When to Fast

Fasting was so engrained in Jewish culture that the Bible doesn't spend much time telling us *how* to fast. The original audiences would not have needed those instructions. And no biblical requirements are placed on Christians today that command regular fasting. But we know from the example of Jesus, from the practice of centuries of church leaders, and can learn quickly from personal experience how beneficial this practice is in orienting our hearts toward God. Our freedom in the gospel from a command on when and how long to fast should be considered an opportunity, not an excuse to ignore it altogether.

So does fasting have to involve food? Not necessarily, as we are not under the old law for any spiritual discipline. But it is worth noting that the original sin in Genesis dealt with food. Eve did not have an iPhone or Netflix subscription for God to choose from, but the physicality of food is important to note. Food was the means to determine if Adam and Eve trusted that God had their best interest at heart.

It is also important to note that in fasting from food as Jesus did, it wasn't about abstaining from something he overindulged in. He fasted from something necessary for life. Our cultural habits (i.e., streaming media, iPhone, social media, etc.) are not necessary to life. Giving up a habit that is a negative force in your life is a great practice, but the better word for that would be *abstinence*. Fasting is not about giving up something you have a problem with, it's about trusting God with the very necessity of life.

## Fasting Types

- **Full Fast:** Establish the number of days and drink only liquids. Start small and work your way up as you feel called.
- **Partial Fast:** Fast from waking until dinner or from sunup to sundown.
- **Daniel Fast:** Eat no meat, sweets, bread, alcohol, or caffeine. Drink only water and juice. Eat fruits and vegetables. (Dan. 1:8–14)

### *Tips to Begin*

Pray over your intentions and goals. Talk with God about why you are fasting and what you are seeking from him. Ask the Holy Spirit for guidance. Confess your sins to God and ask him to reveal weaknesses in your life and people you need to forgive.

Decide the logistics and time and type of fast and give yourself grace as you begin. Try not to have too many expectations and focus on seeking God as your primary goal. Be prepared to experience headaches and irritability as your body withdraws from caffeine or sugar and begins eliminating toxins. Take it easy with physical activity and activities that make you feel emotionally drained or checked out. Engage with God in nature, music, and prayer as much as possible.

### *Ideas for Families*

This practice gives families the opportunity to say together, "Jesus, we want to be closer to you and understand you better." It is telling ourselves and testifying to each other that our top desire is to follow Christ and become more like him. If your children are young, asking them to skip meals may not make sense. In those cases, choose to abstain from something constant in their routine and replace it with connection and reliance on God. Ideas include:

- Abstaining from media and entertainment one night a week for family time.
- Giving up foods associated with feasting like chocolate, desserts, and favorite drinks one day a week. Celebrate God's goodness together as you break the fast with something you enjoy.
- On the same day each week, fast from afternoon snacks and have a late "feast" meal together of something everyone loves, with dessert being a must.

## Individual Practice

**Week One:** If you are physically able, fast from one meal during week one, and during that time, pray for each person in your group by name. If you struggle with fasting from food, abstain from something else that feels essential in your life for a notable amount of time and see how your soul responds. The practices that work best are the ones that connect us to God.

When you feel hungry, pause, breathe deeply, and let it remind you that you are connected to God in your body and even in your hunger. Let your hunger be a prayer to God, expressing your deepest desire for communion with him and relying on him for your deepest physical and spiritual needs. To help you look outward, donate what you would have spent on food to a local shelter and pray for your neighbors who will benefit from it.

As you explore these practices further, consider fasting the day before you experience Sabbath, and observe how the blessing of food from God's good world becomes all the more beautiful and meaningful after a day of fasting.

### In Community

*Group Prayer Prompts*

**Week One:** Fasting is praying with our whole bodies. With that in mind, ask two group members to pray for your time together as you all kneel, lie down, or bow in a physical posture that helps direct your mind and whole body toward the time together.

**Week Two:** Repeat the week one prayer prompt.

*Group Practice*

**Week Two:** Pick twenty-four hours to fast as a group. If at all possible, let this be a fast from food, but if it is not possible for health reasons, members are free to choose something else they engage in multiple times throughout the day.

At consistent intervals during the fast, assign each group member a time to send out a group message with a Scripture they have chosen. This will serve as a way to come together and draw strength and encouragement from the community. Look forward to the times of Scripture reading as you would a good meal. Pray for the person who sent the Scripture as you read it.

If possible, end the day with a meal together. Pray and thank God for the work he is doing in each of your hearts and share your experiences.

*Group Discussion*

**Week One**

1. What stood out to you in the chapter and/or the Scripture readings?
2. Have you ever fasted and what was your experience like?
3. What are some misconceptions you have had or heard about fasting?

**Week Two**

1. How did the week one practice of fasting go? Share some of your experiences.
2. Of the purposes shared in the New and Old Testaments (God's presence, will, wisdom, strength, forgiveness), which one resonates with you the most in this season?
3. If you had a chance to get into the Go Deeper material, what stood out to you?

**Go Deeper**

Practicing the Way: Fasting, particularly episodes 1 and 2 of the podcast

*Revival Starts Here: A Short Conversation on Prayer, Fasting, and Revival for Beginners Like Me*, Dave Clayton

"The Place of Fasting in the Christian Life," Thomas Tarrants, C. S. Lewis Institute

For direct links, visit www.pvcc.org/resources.

## Practice Six

# SABBATH

I REMEMBER A SPECIFIC TIME when I felt overly burdened by what I perceived as the yoke of Christ. I served in many areas in my local church and kids' school, all while trying to figure out how to disciple my family toward Jesus, love my neighbors well, and reach out to strangers. Almost in tears, I told a close friend I must be doing something wrong because Jesus's words in Matthew 11:28, "Come to me, all you who are weary and burdened, and I will give you rest," felt so far away. My love for God and relationship with him were growing, but I felt anything but light and well-rested.

My experience is not uncommon. I can think of very few people who have a posture of restfulness. In the West, we often assume a hurried existence is a way of life. We rush from one commitment to another, and even when we do have a moment to ourselves, our minds and bodies are so burned out that we scroll (literally) through distraction after distraction. We are too tired to give our full attention to anything meaningful and miss the people around us completely.

**Read and Meditate on**
Exodus 20:8–11; Deuteronomy 5:12–15; Psalm 62:1–8; Matthew 11:28–30; 2 Corinthians 4:16–18; Hebrews 4:9–11

The practice of Sabbath pushes back. It is one of the most countercultural and most beautiful invitations we can accept from the way of Jesus. In my experience, it can also be the hardest and most rewarding of the practices. When practiced well, it allows us to experience the love of God on a deeper level and, in turn, to become people who have the time and capacity to love well.

> Hurry is not just a disordered schedule; it's a disordered heart.
> **—John Ortberg,** *The Life You've Always Wanted*[1]

## What Is Sabbath?

Biblical rest is established in the very beginning of the first book of the Bible with two different Hebrew words for rest. In Genesis 2, God blesses the seventh day and makes it holy because, on it, God rested (*shabbat*) from the completed work of creation. Then, a few verses later, he "rests" or "settles" (*nuakh*) humans into the garden with him. Genesis 2 communicates a link between the concepts of *shabbat* and *nuakh*. God rests from work and then dwells with his people. In doing so, he creates a picture of what it means to biblically rest: stop what we are doing and abide in him.

Look back at the verses from Matthew 11 and then read 12:1–14. I don't think it's a coincidence that Matthew follows the promise of a light yoke with two stories about Sabbath. Jesus is inviting us into a way of life that transcends the pressures and responsibilities that weigh us down. He does not require that we retreat to life in a monastery; he is showing how to become people who embody a peaceful, restful spirit in the middle of our busy lives.

Weekly Sabbath rest was fully embedded into Jewish life, culture, and community. The *Mishnah*, considered the first comprehensive written collection of Jewish oral tradition, addresses thirty-nine major categories (with hundreds of subcategories) of labor forbidden on the Sabbath. During Jesus's years of public teaching, he takes a lot of heat from the other rabbis for not following these laws to the letter. Yet he doesn't instruct his followers to ignore the Sabbath. He teaches them to receive it as the gift it truly is and not let it burden them.

In summary, Sabbath is:

- a holy day, set apart by God.
- a day we are charged with keeping holy.
- the *first thing* God made holy.
- more than just a day; it is a way of being in the world.
- a spirit of restfulness that comes from living in the Father's restful presence all week long.
- saying that your ordinary life is enough.
- a weekly reminder that there is a God and that God is not me.
- a gift, not an obligation.
- a reminder that we are more than what we do.
- a reminder that there is more to life than accumulation and accomplishment.
- not a passive discipline. In its practice, you are actively standing in rebellion against culture, proclaiming, "My soul belongs to God alone."
- praying with your schedule, just like fasting is praying with your body.

**Why Is Sabbath So Important?**

Anxiety, exhaustion, and feeling generally overwhelmed physically alert us that something is out of whack spiritually. As stress in our bodies begins to build, it is a signal we should pay close attention to. When we refuse to accept and live within our limitations, we are headed down a road of lasting anxiety and burnout. When we feel this way week after week, we simply cannot love others and follow Jesus well. Habitually worn-out humans do not make effective disciple-makers.

Practicing the Sabbath brings the rest we need to our body, soul, and mind to help us become the loving, joyful, and peaceful beings God created us to be. Sometimes burnout is just about us doing too much. We can fix it by taking a long vacation or sabbatical. But the chronic burnout that more and more of our society is dealing with today, across generations, comes from trying to give something that is not ours to give. It results from refusing to accept the gift of our God-given limitations.

It is common to see our giftings and abilities as gifts from God, but what about our limitations? What if we could begin to view our limitations as gifts of grace in our lives? Sabbath forces us to recognize and honor the limitations of our existence as human beings. As we do this, something deeply spiritual begins to happen. After all, if catching up worked, don't you think you'd be caught up by now?

If our goal as followers of Christ is to be more like him and to grow in love for God and each other, why are we so driven to achieve money, attention, success, financial security, and physical comfort? Why are we so afraid to follow the example of Jesus, letting go of our illusion of control and simply resting in the love and goodness of God?

Sometimes our desire for certain levels of achievement, accolade, improved lifestyle, or even passion for an area of service or ministry will drive us and keep us from resting. But for some, the need to continue our work is one of distraction. Overworking and overscheduling our calendars keep us from facing what is wrong in our hearts and lives. So we push through, day in and day out, losing sight of the joy God longs to give us by simply resting in him.

> God invites us into a rhythm where he is our deep breath. Time in rest fortifies us for the fight and the life he's called us to.
>
> **—Beth Guckenberger,** *Throw the First Punch*[2]

What would your life be like if you were courageous enough to trust God's good gift of the Sabbath once every week? What would change in how you viewed and walked in the world the other six days if you knew your time of rest with God, the Creator of the universe, was coming?

John Mark Comer suggests that when we move beyond talking about the Sabbath into practicing it, its goodness begins to take over. He remarks that on Sabbath, deep, meaningful rest turns into simple joy and delight in the food, people, and activities you are enjoying, the delight turns into gratitude as you reflect on the goodness of God, and the gratitude turns into worship in song, prayer, or heart posture. This transition is not seamless and will not progress perfectly every time you give Sabbath a try. But if you stick with it, soon enough it will capture your body, mind, and soul and leave you wanting more.[3]

### Is Sabbath for Everyone?

As disciples of Jesus, our call is much bigger than our personal, private practices. We must also look out as disciple-makers and ask: Can Sabbath really be for everyone, or is it just for those with the means and privilege to take advantage of it?

Sabbath was also created for the *whole* community of God, not just those with the economic privilege to participate. It reminds

God's people that none of us should live as slaves to a people group, to our culture, or to our jobs.

In *The New Testament in Color* commentary, Miguel Echevarria notes how much Jesus cared about the disparities in the physical world, citing John 1:5–6, 5:35, and 1:7. "Jesus came 'in the flesh' to give humanity fullness of life on earth," he writes. When we work through racial and economic barriers toward a goal of human flourishing for all people, Echevarria would say we are creating a witness "that brightens a dark world, beckoning others to follow the God who is shining His renewing light into the darkness."[4] In our wildly individualistic culture, it is hard to wrap our minds around how to create a space of Sabbath for a whole community. But as people bearing witness to the renewal of all things to come, it is an important challenge to wrestle with. This tension is ever-present as we try to live as Christians in the now and the not-yet of the kingdom of God.

Recognizing this challenge is also vital to our spiritual formation. A few helpful questions to ask ourselves as we begin to feel the benefit of a regular Sabbath practice are: Who in my community is tired and weary? How can I provide moments of rest to help lighten their load? It could be that the only "work" involved in Sabbath is to make sure our neighbors can also rest well.

## How to Begin

Start by throwing out all the assumed rules and all the reasons this practice won't work for you. Remember Jesus's words in Mark 2:27, "Sabbath was made for man, not man for the Sabbath." Start with a clean slate and an open mind.

> To practice Sabbath we have to know what we are in bondage to, what has us in its grip, and that is precisely the thing we should cease. We need to know what wears us out and wears us down, what robs us of our joy and peace and cease that. Because that is exactly what God wants to free us from.
>
> —**Ruth Haley Barton,** *Sacred Rhythms*[5]

*Establish Your Rhythm*

When will you start? Do your very best to pick the same day or portion of a day each week. Make it a priority. A floating Sabbath based on your schedule can sometimes be necessary, but when the day on the calendar itself is not a priority, and there has to be a decision each week as to when it will happen, you are robbing Sabbath of its power over your life.

Very few people have a day each week that naturally stays open without obligations, appointments, and commitments. Sacrifices will have to be made, but give yourself the grace to navigate this over time. Don't expect to be able to make it work perfectly in the beginning.

Keep trying. If needed, try a half day or even an hour or two. If something comes up that is draining but just cannot be avoided—for me, that would be running to the store or taking a kid to a birthday party—try not to be frustrated or discouraged. Instead, go with a heart posture of gratitude and love for the people God put in your community.

Ruth Haley Barton tells a great story about when her daughter played high school soccer. If she had a game on the day Ruth and her husband practiced Sabbath, the daughter knew that that day was different and that mom would not be at the game. Six days a week, Ruth ran her kids to practices and games, but on the seventh, they found their own ride. That may sound crazy to most parents today, but it is a powerful example of putting spiritual formation first to grow in love for God and others, including our children. Ruth's daughter is now grown and an avid Sabbath practicer along with her husband and small children, not a professional soccer player. She speaks on Ruth's podcast of the importance of seeing her parents take this discipline seriously and the long-term difference it made in their family.[7]

*Form Your Sabbath*

The following four rhythms are adapted from the *Rule of Life* podcast created by Practicing the Way.[6] Use them as a guideline to help organize and support your Sabbath time.

1. **Stop.** Cease working, worrying, and wanting things. Let the housework, career work, and schoolwork be done for twenty-four hours, even if they aren't. Use your own definition of "work." Does the actual activity (not just the satisfaction of having it done) fill me up or drain me? Does it bring me joy or frustration? Does it bring me peace or anxiety? Trust God to be in control of your life and the world around you. Here are other ideas to consider:

   - Work toward giving up shopping for the day, preparing ahead for groceries, and allowing your soul a day to be content with what you have. Recognize the need to move toward a world where service workers and shopkeepers can enjoy a time of rest as well.
   - Light a candle to mark the beginning of the Sabbath. As it burns, speak the things left to do and allow the cares and anxiety associated with them to melt away, knowing God has them under control.
   - Keep a Sabbath journal. Write down the cares, worries, and things left undone as a prayer of trust that God will

provide. When you revisit the journal the following week, praise God for his thoughtful care over your life. You can also keep your journal, devices, and anything else that symbolizes work, want, and worry in a special Sabbath box. Getting it out and filling it up each week can serve as an intentional beginning point of the Sabbath.

- Read or pray a Psalm. Traditionally, Psalms 95–99, Psalm 29, and Psalm 92 are all read to begin the Sabbath.

2. **Rest.** Do things that fill you up and leave you rested and energized. Linger over a meal, have an extra cup of coffee in your favorite spot, nap, read a good book, explore your creative side, and do something you'd not normally take time for in a busy week. Let your whole body fully relax, and pay attention to how that feels. Some weeks it might take longer than others to physically and mentally decompress from the level of productivity you experience throughout the week.

3. **Delight.** Look for the God-given beauty around you—in nature, art, music, and each other. Enjoy good food, drink, sex (if you are married), and good times around the table. Sabbath is best enjoyed with the closest of family and friends—the kind of people you don't have to clean up for. This will not always be possible for everyone, but inviting people you love into your Sabbath is a goal worth working toward.

   Remember that there is a difference between delight and indulgence. The Sabbath was made holy by God, and we are to keep it holy. If we are not careful, it can become a day to justify indulgence, whether that's drinking too much, eating too much, or indulging in selfish behavior that does not honor the Sabbath for those around us. True delight should always point our hearts toward gratitude for God and all he has done for us, not shift our focus inwardly on personal indulgence.

4. **Worship.** Take the time to let your gaze settle on your Creator and his good world. Let your whole day be an act of worship as you develop a heart that is looking for God in ordinary moments as well as spectacular ones. Praise God with your words and your heart posture all day long. Continually pray short prayers of thanksgiving for the things you delight in, whether it's beauty in nature, a meal, a laugh, or something beautiful you notice in someone around you.

   If you struggle to keep your focus on God, try setting reminders throughout the day to read a Psalm, listen to worship music, or pray a prayer of thanksgiving—whatever activity will reorient your heart to focus on God's goodness. If you practice Sabbath on a day your local church gathers, give your full self in worship with your community.

## Special Circumstances

Every initial conversation about the practice of sabbath that I have had eventually gets around to the question, "What about . . .?" Our minds cannot help but jump to the what ifs when we consider altering our routines in a big way. I'll address a few of the most common below, but remember to give yourself grace as you figure out what brings you and your family lasting rest.

### *Parents with Kids at Home*

If you have children in the home, they must see the Sabbath as a gift and not a burden for it to be successful. If they are in preschool or early elementary school, develop fun routines for everyone (play their favorite games, eat their favorite foods, give special privileges, etc.), but also allow for time during the day for parents to relax. Spouses can take turns sleeping in, taking naps, or slipping away to read a book. Single parents and couples can utilize sitters or family, if not weekly, at least occasionally, or finally say yes to letting that trusted older person at church or in your neighborhood babysit for a few hours. A little extra screen time can also be incorporated to give parents an extra break to refuel. Remember, this is the exception, not the everyday rule—give yourself grace.

If your children are older, tread carefully and don't force it. Let them see the joy the Sabbath brings you over time and then invite them into it. No matter how old your kids are, food is key! Delight in good food and time around the table, or enjoy a special dessert while watching a movie. Say yes as much as possible to the things that bring them joy and bring you closer together.

*Screens or No Screens?*

This is a decision you need to make considering how your family relates to and uses technology daily. Having regular breaks from screens is vital from a secular and spiritual standpoint when discussing healthy lifestyle habits (a few great books on this are *The Tech–Wise Family* by Andy Crouch and *The Anxious Generation* by Jonathan Hiadt[7]). But if you focus too much on Sabbath being about turning off devices, especially with kids, it can quickly become more about what you can't do that day instead of the gift of rest. Ask yourself and your family why you hesitate to put your phones away. Is it about entertainment? Distraction? Do you feel you are needed and cannot miss a call or text? Prayerfully consider those and other questions alongside the goals to stop, rest, delight, and worship to come up with what works for your family.

*No "Job"?*

If you are retired from working, a stay-at-home parent, or someone who does not have a paid job with responsibilities to an employer, begin by creating your definition of work and rest. Prayerfully consider what fills you and points your heart toward gratitude for God. Also, consider what drains you or fills you with anxiety or dread. Then build your day around those life-giving activities. A simple example would be how you feel after an hour of scrolling your phone or watching something on TV compared to reading a good book. Look for things that fill your soul and create gratitude for God and his good world.

There are many other traditions and resources that can be learned from the Jewish faith and Christian writers. See the notes in the Go Deeper section for a place to start. Don't overthink it! A successful Sabbath simply results in giving and receiving God's love, which, over time, transforms your heart as you begin to live from it all week long.

## Individual Practice

**Week One:** Pick a day or half a day to practice Sabbath in the coming week. Prepare for it throughout the week, both physically by doing anything that needs to be done and spiritually by preparing your heart in prayer.

Pray for each member of your group by name.

Keep working on it! Adjust if needed, give yourself grace, and try again.

**Week Two:** Pray for each member of your group by name.

## In Community

*Group Prayer Prompt*

**Week One:** Have everyone write the following prayer, or their own prayer, to recite before beginning their Sabbath. This one is adapted from the Jewish *Kiddush* prayer, which has been part of the Jewish Sabbath since the sixth and fourth centuries BCE. You can light a candle when saying "Let this light represent."

> Let us welcome the Sabbath with joy and peace. Let us put aside our work, wants and worry and delight in the goodness of God and the blessing of rest. Let this light represent the love of God in our home. Amen.

**Week Two:** Spend a few minutes in silent meditation considering any personal roadblocks or hesitations you have toward practicing the Sabbath regularly. Have each group member write them down on a slip of paper and place them all in the middle of the circle. Have a group member pray that God will give us all the wisdom and faith to trust him enough to overcome these roadblocks and continue trying in this discipline.

*Group Discussion*

**Week One**

1. What stood out to you in the chapter and/or the Scripture readings?
2. Have you ever practiced Sabbath? If so, how did it go?
3. Read the Ruth Haley Barton quote on page 99. What are you in bondage to now? What is weighing you down and stressing you out?
4. What area of your life feels the most hurried and busy? Is it seasonal or chronic?
5. How can you accept God's invitation to rest practically?

**Week Two**

1. How did the week one practice of Sabbath go? Share some of your experiences.

2. How do you think practicing this intentional time of rest forms our hearts to be more like Jesus? How does it make us more loving?
3. What is the biggest change you will have to make to try this for a few weeks?
4. If you had a chance to get into the Go Deeper material, what stood out to you?

**Go Deeper**

*Rule of Life* podcast, John Mark Comer, episodes for Stop, Rest, Delight, and Worship

*Sacred Rhythms: Arranging Our Lives for Spiritual Transformation,* Ruth Haley Barton, Chapter 8

*Subversive Sabbath: The Surprising Power of Rest in a Nonstop World,* A. J. Swoboda

*The Tech-Wise Family: Everyday Steps for Putting Technology in Its Proper Place,* Andy Crouch

*Sabbath Companion Guide* and *Sabbath Meditations,* Practicing the Way

*Our Unforming: De-Westernizing Spiritual Formation,* Cindy S. Lee, Chapter 6

*Sabbath Keeping: Finding Freedom in the Rhythms of Rest,* Lynne M. Baab

For direct links, visit www.pvcc.org/resources.

# Practice Seven

## CONFESSION AND FORGIVENESS

A CHILD IS CAUGHT. He and his parents know what he did and that it was wrong, how it hurt others, and how it went against the parents' instruction. It was a simple misstep that is part of growing up. But no matter what his parents say or do to reassure their son that he is loved and will be forgiven, he will not admit the obvious fault. He digs in. Fearful of punishment and full of pride and shame, he will not confess. He will not simply admit his mistake and accept the freedom and redemption found on the other side of reconciliation.

From the vantage point of a parent or teacher, this scenario is maddening. Surely, if the child could only see what we see and how deeply we long to put things right for them, they would come clean. Surely they would confess and accept the gift of grace offered by their parent, who loves them and only wants to help them make a better choice in the future. How many times are we as adults caught in the same situation? How often do we let big and small things stand between us and reconciled friendship? And more so, how often do we let our inability to confess sin keep us from lasting change and from a deeper relationship with God?

We know that God is love, and he longs to show us his love through the gift of forgiveness. God's immense love for us brought

Jesus to the cross, not his anger over our sins. So why are we so afraid of our brokenness? After all, the fundamental principle of the Christian faith is that we are broken, and Christ came to make us whole.

**Read and Meditate on**
Leviticus 5:5, 13; Matthew 18:21–35; Mark 1:15; Ephesians 4:32; Colossians 3:13; James 5:16; 2 Corinthians 5:14–21

## Confession

Confession has long been one of the core practices of followers of God. Even before Jesus, Jews practiced confession, penance, and the remission of sins, as shown in Leviticus 5 and throughout the Old Testament. Confession and the life it brings are beautiful gifts from God available to all of us from the beginning. So, what keeps us from accepting it?

Sometimes we are just like the child, fearful of, or already suffering from, the shame of where we have failed and worried that confession will only amplify the pain we would rather avoid. We cannot even be honest with ourselves about our sins, much less share them with a close friend or mentor. We fear how we will be seen, how others will react, and how their perception of us might be altered.

Sometimes we are unable to recognize our sins. We go to church and sing about our thankfulness to God for our salvation, but if we are truly honest, we don't really think we have anything to confess. After all, we have done all the right things, checked all the right boxes, and avoided the public disgrace. Maybe our sins are so socially acceptable or even encouraged enough by culture that we have stopped seeing them for what they are.

If this is the case, we have to open our eyes as disciples. Regardless of the offense, a life without confession robs the cross of its transformative power over us. Confession is not meant to be something we avoid or a burden we carry. Just like the other disciplines, confession is an invitation we need to accept. Without it, we limit our capacity to grow in our relationship with God and others.

In her book on spiritual warfare, *Throw the First Punch*, author Beth Guckenberger draws a connection between our lack of confession and our limited capacity to carry out God's will in our lives: "With grieving [over sin]and confession came the unintended benefit of capacity. I want more capacity because capacity increases my impact. When I [confess and] am not carrying what isn't mine to carry, I have more room in my heart and hands to hold what God entrusts to me."[1]

I think it's safe to say that we'd all sign up for more capacity. As our relationship with Jesus grows deeper, he will reveal more and more of our hearts' inner workings and sinfulness. It is then up to us to overcome the fear and pride that prevent us from accepting God's invitation to confession and repentance. Over time, we can learn to trust him in this life-giving practice, not to get him off our backs, but to continually walk with him in freedom. As Trevor Hudson writes in *Seeking God*, "Repentance is not only the doorway into the life God gives; it is also the pathway along which we need to walk throughout our lives."[2]

My grandmother was a wonderful gardener. Some of my earliest memories with her are of shelling purple hull peas on her mother's back porch. We were very close, and when she passed away, I was inspired to take up the mantle as a way to feel close to her. I upped my gardening game from a few pots to tilling up the entire back corner of my yard with an ancient gas-powered tiller I found on Facebook Marketplace. I love old things and finding deals, so this was right up my alley.

Unfortunately, I did not receive her green thumb in my genetic code and am terrible at gardening. I've never harvested enough of anything to even feed my family for one meal. But that rusty tiller, now quiet and covered in weeds in my backyard, is an apt reminder of how God has shown me the beauty and freedom found in confession over time.

As I have grown deeper with God through all these practices, I have been surprised at what has been unearthed in my heart. Like soil being turned over and over, time in silence and solitude, time fasting, and time spent deep in Scripture have revealed many things that had gone unnoticed for years. Motives that needed to be addressed, emotions that needed healing, and secret sins that needed to see the light of day to help me grow into the person I hope one day to be.

Before walking with God through this process, I would have expected to feel burdened and guilty about drudging up these things that had long gone unchecked. But instead, I felt joy. Even sharing these things in a small group setting brought relief—not just to have them off my chest but through the realization that when I was honest with myself and others before God, I could really change.

Each time we confess, turn from our sin, and accept the healing God is waiting to provide, we are freed to walk away from the heaviness of guilt and shame and into a life of purpose and reconciliation. Then we, in turn, can become reconcilers through forgiveness as Paul prompts us to in Ephesians 4:32.

## Forgiveness

Forgiveness begins with being forgiven. When we fully recognize our brokenness and the joy of being forgiven, we are free to humble ourselves and open our hearts in forgiveness to others. Being able to forgive is one of the most powerful ways we live out the love of Christ. Culture will push back against this and urge us to protect our interests and fight for justice, but for the disciple, mercy is greater than judgment (James 2:13). There is simply no better way to live. Christians know this to be true; but it is still difficult to let go.

I used to think forgiveness was easier than confession. I think that is because I like to be right, and forgiveness lets me be the bigger person. But then I had something happen in my life that was truly hard to forgive. A close friend unexpectedly hurt me and then lied about it multiple times. On the surface, it wasn't even that big of a deal. Her actions would not change my life in any real way or cause lasting harm, but the situation ate away at my soul. No matter what I said or did on the outside to put it behind me, it wouldn't go away and was ruining a relationship that otherwise could have been life-giving.

Unforgiveness makes us feel cold, angry, bitter, and resentful. Even when we are completely justified in our anger, failing to fully forgive is crippling. Jesus describes the consequences of unforgiveness like torture in Matthew 18:21–35. The king in the parable wants to forgive his servant but cannot because the servant cannot offer the same grace to others. The unforgiving servant ends up imprisoned and tortured. Jesus illustrates the self-inflicted pain that unforgiveness adds to an already hurtful situation. You could compare it to the often quoted truth, "Unforgiveness is like drinking poison and hoping the other person dies."

God does not want us to carry this burden. He gives us free will to choose between anger and resentment or freedom and love, and he sent Jesus to show us how it could be done. Jesus lavishes grace and mercy on us freely and waits to see if we will be willing to simply reflect it back to others—to freely give as we have freely received.

Forgiveness is so essential to our mental and physical health that it is widely discussed and recommended by psychologists, counselors, and medical doctors. The Mayo Clinic cites depression, anxiety, high blood pressure, and low self-esteem among many of the health risks of holding a grudge. They offer practical advice like joining a support group, journaling, releasing the control and power the offending person has over your life, practicing empathy by trying to see things from the other person's point of view, and asking yourself about the circumstances that led them to behave in this way.

For Christians, forgiveness begins with prayer to enlist the help of the Holy Spirit. Look back at the Lord's Prayer from Matthew 6:9–13 and remember that these words were given daily: "Forgive our debts, as we also have forgiven our debtors." Daily prayer to be forgiven and to forgive is essential in the life of a disciple. Bring the person who hurt you to God in prayer every day. Ask God to help him or her heal and be forgiven, and petition God to help you forgive as well. Seek the best for them in prayer. Ask that you will begin to see the person through God's eyes as his child. Ask for blessings of peace over their lives and that their desire to know God will grow alongside your own.

This will not be easy. Remember from Ephesians 6:12 that "our struggle is not against flesh and blood, but against the rulers, against the authorities, against the powers of this dark world and against the spiritual forces of evil in the heavenly realms." All the pain and hurt you feel does not have to stay attached to a person or circumstance. Remember that dark forces are actively at work trying to keep you bitter, angry, and resentful.

Our world will stay broken this side of heaven. We will continue to offend and hurt each other, ranging in everything from minor annoyances to life-altering, generational trauma. But the disciple always has the choice to accept God's invitation to separate an action from a person. To no longer suffer under the weight of resentment and to instead walk in mercy and love.

While Christ calls us to forgive, it is important to note that forgiveness does not mean forgetting, and it doesn't always lead to reconciliation with the person who hurt you. It does not require you to let that person back into your life or even forgo any necessary consequences, legal or otherwise.

Forgiveness is in the hands and heart of the person who was hurt. It requires that they acknowledge the offense, but they choose to no longer define the offender by it. Reconciliation, on the other hand, is not called for or even healthy in every situation. It requires both offender and victim to recognize the offense and share the cost of making things right again. This cannot and should not always happen in cases of deep hurts and abuse. The paths to forgiveness and reconciliation, and how they are lived out, will be very different depending on the offense and the people involved.

> What every forgiveness story does hold in common, though, is this, taking up your cross. Football games between 8-year-olds and 12-year-marriage stories. Abuse and betrayal, petty gossip, and angry outbursts. To cancel any debt, big or small, simple or complex, fast or slow, requires the act of suffering of cross bearing.
>
> **—Tyler Staton,** "How Many Times Should I Forgive?"[3]

Forgiveness is also not just a one-time event. Most often, we have to keep choosing it. It is a process. Even small hurts may need to be revisited and forgiven repeatedly.

**Individual Practice**

Return to the prayer of examen in Practice Two. Every day this week and next, enter into this practice before you go to bed, paying special attention to the prompts to confess and forgive. When something comes up that you need to confess to someone else, either to help you rest in the freedom of God's forgiveness or because you need to ask forgiveness of another person, don't wait. Reach out to that person via text or plan right then when and where you will reconcile that relationship.

Pray for each member of your group by name each week.

### In Community

> A man who confesses his sins in the presence of a brother knows that he is no longer alone with himself; he experiences the presence of God in the reality of the other person. As long as I am by myself in the confession of my sins, everything remains in the dark, but in the presence of a brother, the sin has to be brought into the light.
>
> —**Dietrich Bonhoeffer,** *Life Together*[4]

*Group Prayer Prompts*

**Week One:** Begin your time together by practicing a modified examen prayer. Encourage group members to be as transparent as possible, emphasizing the importance of being open with each other and trusting the confidentiality of the group.

Take a moment to recognize the presence of the Holy Spirit and ask that presence to reveal the truth in the hearts of group members. Then go around the circle and let each person pray out loud, confessing a regret from the day or week before. It could be anything they wish they had done differently or an opportunity they missed to act in love.

As you pray, simply ask for forgiveness, and as you confess, remember that the love of God is always with you and within you.

After each person speaks, the group will respond, "Lord, hear our prayer and forgive." If someone does not have a specific confession they are willing or able to make, let them feel free to just say, "Lord, please forgive my brokenness." They may also pray for help to forgive something hard to let go of.

**Week Two:** Have a group member pray for the forgiveness God offers us freely. End with three to five minutes of silence, meditating individually on this prayer: "God, thank you for helping me to see who you have made me to be and who you are helping me to become." Consider what action you would like to take tomorrow that will help you fulfill God's vision for your life.

*Group Discussion*

**Week One**

1. What stood out to you in the chapter and/or the Scripture readings?
2. St. Alphonsus Liguori, an Italian Bishop, wrote in the 1700s that for a good confession, three things are necessary: an examination of conscience, sorrow, and a determination to avoid sin. Which of those steps is the hardest for you, and has that answer differed based on the situation you found yourself in?
3. Share a time in your life, big or small, when forgiveness was difficult for you. Was it resolved or is it still a scar you carry?

**Week Two**

1. How did the week one practice of confession and forgiveness go? Share some of your experiences.
2. 1 Peter 2:9 tells us we are a royal priesthood that can forgive each other (or withhold forgiveness). Have you experienced that kind of relationship in the church before, either in an official capacity with a church leader or relationally with a close friend or mentor?

3. Hopefully throughout your time together in this group, you have shared ways you have been hurt and have hurt others. What has happened to you recently? What sins do you have that still linger? Is there an ongoing struggle or need to forgive in your life that you have not yet shared with the group? If not to the whole group, seek out one member this week to receive your confession and pray for your freedom, trusting the words of 1 John 1:9 that "he is faithful and just and will forgive us our sins and purify us from all unrighteousness."
4. If you had a chance to get into the Go Deeper material, what stood out to you?

## Go Deeper

"Changing Direction," video with Trevor Hudson

*Seeking God: Finding Another Kind of Life with St. Ignatius and Dallas Willard,* Trevor Hudson, Chapter 2

*The Cure: What If God Isn't Who You Think He Is and Neither Are You?*, John Lynch, Bruce McNicol, and Bill Thrall

"The Power of Confession," *Strengthening the Soul of Your Leadership* podcast, Ruth Haley Barton, season 15, Lent week 4

*Celebration of Discipline: The Path to Spiritual Growth,* Richard Foster, Chapter 10

"Forgiveness—Gospel of Matthew Part 26," *Exploring My Strange Bible* podcast

Forgiving as We Have Been Forgiven, four-part sermon series on forgiveness, Bridgetown Church in Portland, Oregon, March 2018.

*The RobCast* podcast with Rob Bell, episodes 38–42.

"For the Sake of Others: How Many Times Should I Forgive?," *Bridgetown Audio Podcast,* November 18, 2024

*I Want to Move On: Break Free from Bitterness and Discover Freedom in Forgiveness*, Lauren Vander Linden

For direct links, visit www.pvcc.org/resources.

# Practice Eight

## GENEROSITY

A COUPLE I'VE KNOWN AND respected for a long time, we'll call them the Joneses, have been incredibly gifted by God, each in their unique way. They were very successful in their careers. They used their talents for God's glory, and he blessed them in every way. They have more than enough money to cover their needs and are well-respected in the community and their professional arenas. They likely could have climbed even higher in their respective areas, but they chose a different route.

They made career and life choices that allowed them the time and money to serve their local community and global efforts in meaningful and long-lasting ways. They sacrificed over and over to the point that it was their way of life to put others first.

Over the decades, they did not grow their standard of living with the growth of their paychecks. They maintained the same home they bought when their children were young, shopped in secondhand stores, and drove older used cars. They took the time to disciple others and pour physical and financial resources into some of our world's most needy areas. Years after many of their peers have retired and retreated, they are still at work building a legacy that will only be fully realized in heaven.

They are undoubtedly well-loved and respected, but one thing about their story bothers me. Instead of being an inspiration for all of us to keep up with, many in our church family view the Joneses as if they were wired differently than you and me. There seems to be an unspoken assumption that they live the way they do because they are different, and not, as Jesus suggests, that they are different because of the radically generous way they live.

They model Jesus-style generosity, stewarding their entire lives—their time, money, talents, and even purchasing choices—to honor God and bless others. Their lives tell the gospel's good news through generosity in a million tiny ways and in large, sacrificial ways. They are bringing the kingdom of heaven to earth right now.

**Read and Meditate on**
Deuteronomy 8:18; 1 Chronicles 29:12–14; Matthew 6:19–24; Matthew 25:34–40; Luke 3:10–11; Luke 6:30–31; Luke 12:23–24; Luke 16:13; Acts 2:42–47; and 1 John 3:17–18

## The Elephant in the Room

If you've been around church very long, you likely have heard about how much Jesus teaches on money, but you may not have heard many sermons on it. It's an awkward subject because it feels subjective and invasive, and thanks to cringy televangelists, it causes suspicion anytime it's brought up on a Sunday morning. So, the default for many churches seems to be to leave it alone, apart from a few giving pushes late in the year to make the annual budget.

Depending on who you ask, Jesus uses about 15 to 25 percent of his teaching time to address our relationship with money, a topic he never views positively, unless he's asking us to give it away. In Matthew 6:24 and Luke 16:9, 11, and 13, the word used for money and wealth is the Aramaic word *mammon*. The word itself is not inherently evil as it just means "wealth or possessions." But by comparing mammon to a master, Jesus is warning us that regardless of what we want to believe, money is not neutral. It has the power to control our lives. Over time, mammon became synonymous with a powerful demon of extreme greed and pagan gods in the Middle Ages.

Jesus wants something better for you than chasing and being controlled by the god of more. Have you noticed that even though Jesus speaks about money often, he never asks for it? Because Jesus is not after your money; he is always after your heart. Our relationship with money is a window into our hearts. What we value, who we trust, where we find security, how patient we are, and more are all laid bare by how we view, spend, and give our money.

To fight the pull of mammon, Jesus invites us into the practice of generosity. When this invitation is accepted, it opens the door to contentment and joy. True contentment means I don't have to reach for the next toy, clothing item, house, job, or drink to feel valued or escape reality. It means that I know who I am in the sight of God, and that is enough.

> The content are those whose joy does not rise and fall based on the acquisition, but instead, they have trained themselves to point their wanting to the source of living water who will finally and fully quench their thirst. And contentment is the base from which I can freely love others.
>
> **—Tyler Staton,** "For the Sake of the Poor"[1]

### What Was Jesus *Really* Saying?

Jesus makes very clear, bold declarations about what we do with our money, yet so few of us take him at his word. In Luke 18, a young ruler whom we can assume is wealthy and powerful approaches Jesus. He has kept the Jewish commandments all his life and lived up to everyone's expectations of him. We can guess that his parents are proud and he is seen as a success, but something is missing. He comes to Jesus, who sees the nature of his heart and challenges him to leave it all behind. Jesus tells him to give all his wealth to the poor and follow him.

Luke tells us that the man walked away sad, leaving us to believe he was too wrapped up in his possessions to follow Jesus. His trust and security was in the life he built and protected with his wealth.

I can't tell you how many times I have heard that story, and others about wealth, brushed off and explained away as if they do not apply to us. We sometimes like to think that "rich" is just the person with a little more than me, us, or you. We live in a culture that celebrates self-made men and women, and it's become far too normalized to seek self-reliance over trust in God. The more secure we are in our own means, the easier it becomes to ignore what Jesus was getting at.

Before we gear up to explain the hard teachings away, we need to closely examine how the people who heard those hard teachings first- or secondhand responded to them. In Acts 2, we see the early church receiving the Holy Spirit in crazy, powerful ways, baptizing thousands and creating the kind of sacrificially generous community Jesus talked about. It wasn't theory or just for the "radical Christians." Luke tells us in Acts 2:45 and reemphasizes the message in Acts 4:32 that these early followers sold everything they had and shared it all in community. And the community thrived as disciple-makers.

Even if Jesus hadn't told us, we know from observation and life experience that the accumulation of money and stuff does not lead to happiness. We see it all around us in culture, in our families and neighborhoods, and even in the mirror. But we rarely make life decisions that reflect that knowledge. Think for a moment about how we celebrate with each other the promotion, the new car, the new house, the new outfit, the fancy vacation, or the second home. If we are being honest, we celebrate not because a real need was met or because we now have the means to give more, but because we think we are being blessed by becoming more successful. We feel more secure because we have more stuff. We are building bigger barns (see Luke 12:16–21).

If your worldview stems from the individualistic culture of North America, pushing back against the god of accumulation and creating the type of community mentioned in Acts likely seems too idealistic, inconvenient, or just plain socialistic. However, other cultures have long embraced this ideal and have something to teach the rest of us. Filipino culture for example lives out a core value they call *kwapa.* In this way of looking at the world, the elimination of poverty comes not from accumulation but from unity in the way a community relates to one another and pulls each other up.[2]

It is understandably a stretch for most of us to imagine living like the community in Acts today. And the truth is, none of us, including the early Christians, can fully measure up to what Jesus calls for regarding our money. After all, if the rich are the people with a little more than me, the poor are always the people with a little less than me. We are left with a subjective sliding scale where we never measure up. Praise God for grace.

Jesus advocates radical generosity, but as with any practice, it begins with the heart. When we approach the world with an open hand and a content heart, we begin to feel the joy of giving without conditions or judgment. We feel the peace from being able to say, "No, thank you, what I already have will work just fine," or "Yes, we can afford it, but we don't need it," or as I tell my teenage daughters, "Just because it fits and is on sale doesn't mean you have to buy it." Because of Jesus, we can look at all the world has to offer and simply say, "I have enough."

There is great freedom that comes with trusting Jesus in this way. The more we have, the more we worry and fret over it being taken away, and the more time and money we spend maintaining and storing our possessions. Trusting Jesus in living simply and generously really is a pathway to great personal joy and sets our hearts free from so many unnecessary worries, anxieties, and fears.

This heart posture develops slowly over time. According to author and speaker John Mark Comer, your giving has become transformative when you feel the fruit of the Spirit coming alive as you give. When people look at your life and spending habits, they assume you make significantly less than you do. When you quit wondering if you are giving enough and start wondering how much you should keep, Comer would say you are on the right track to the abundant life Jesus wants for you.[3]

And sometimes, even when approaching a situation with a generous heart, there can be a struggle with the line between stewardship and generosity. Biblical stewardship involves faithfully managing all the resources entrusted to us by God. It begins in Genesis 1 when God calls Adam and Eve to be fruitful and rule the earth. As disciples who chose to partner with God on earth, it is important to take responsibility for the resources we have been given and manage them well. But if we are not careful, we limit the concept of biblical stewardship to protecting our money and talk ourselves out of the kind of generosity described in the New Testament.

Most of us want to help the vulnerable and know that it is important to God for us to do so. But if we are honest, we sometimes only want to help the vulnerable who, in our estimation, are somehow worthy of the help. As soon as we get a whiff of someone's bad decisions resulting in their situation, it can be all too easy to get a little less openhanded and a lot more "judgy." Regarding generosity, Jesus doesn't seem to think people must qualify for it. He also doesn't seem to think giving out of our excess while we build our bigger barns on the side will cut it (see again Luke 12:13–21). Jesus-style generosity is much more about living with an open heart and an open hand than who receives our gifts.

### The Debt Effect

According to a 2023 survey conducted by Payroll.org, 78 percent of Americans live paycheck to paycheck, a 6 percent increase from the previous year.[4] In other words, more than three-quarters of Americans struggle to cover essential living expenses like housing, utilities, groceries, and transportation. Giving, saving, and investing are not even a possibility. This scenario puts families at great risk of financial ruin if one paycheck is missed or one emergency or large unexpected expense arises.

Even more concerning was a 2023 study done by Forbes Advisor that reported 29 percent of Americans are making an income that does not even cover their monthly expenses.[5] So where does that leave the Christian who desires to follow Jesus with their giving but never has enough left over?

> "Bring the whole tithe into the storehouse, that there may be food in my house. Test me in this," says the LORD Almighty, "and see if I will not throw open the floodgates of heaven and pour out so much blessing that there will not be room enough to store it." (Mal. 3:10)

This is the only place in Scripture where God says to test him. The Jewish tradition of a tithe, or 10 percent, is a great place to start. What would it look like if you accepted the invitation of generosity? Standard practice says to **live** on your money, then **save** a little, then if there is anything left, **give** some away. What if instead you flipped the script to **give** 10 percent first, then **save** (or pay down debt), and **live** on what was left?

| | | |
|---|---|---|
| LIVE<br>SAVE<br>GIVE | → | GIVE<br>SAVE<br>LIVE |

Depending on your situation, this might seem impossible. If that is where you find yourself, take it a little at a time, and don't get discouraged. Start with 3, 5, or 8 percent. Prayerfully trust God to meet you where you are and help you grow in your desire and financial ability to be a person of radical generosity. Remember that everything you have belongs to God anyway, and steward it accordingly.

**Individual Practice**

**Week One**

> Giving away resources when it makes no sense is a powerful way of showing people that Jesus is truly the risen Lord of the world.
>
> **—Tim Mackie,** "A Generous Gospel"[6]

What if we didn't explain away Jesus's teachings and the community we see in Acts 2 to make them fit our lifestyle? What if we accepted his grace, humbly knowing that we are all falling short but stretching ourselves to grow in our generosity and experience the joy of letting go? Could making intentional decisions to give counterculturally result in life-changing freedom from idols we did not even know we had?

Consider also how the practices work together. Could a weekly Sabbath, practiced over a lifetime, make us into the kind of people who didn't live for retirement? Could it help free us to worry a little less about how big our barns are becoming?

Prayerfully consider one act that feels unusually generous for you. It doesn't have to make a whole lot of sense or be overly thought out, just something outside your normal habits that will bring someone else joy. Maybe it's buying the person in line behind you their coffee for the day or the week, buying or making a friend's dinner unexpectedly, or giving your time to serve in an unexpected way. Or maybe it's keeping a good amount of cash on hand to give to anyone who asks over the next week, to practice the posture of having an open hand. Humbly recognize that the possibility of being taken advantage of in your giving is worth the risk to feel the joy of generosity. Practice gratitude, remembering that none of it was ever yours in the first place.

Maybe it's something even larger, like downsizing your house, giving away a car, or trading down so you can give up a car payment to help someone else. Pray on this over the next two weeks and whatever God puts on your heart. This is not a "health and wealth" gospel message—just follow God and your life will be all sunshine and rainbows. It's a challenge to reexamine your heart and your definition of blessings. Make a plan now to challenge yourself to be countercultural in your giving in the name of Jesus and see if he doesn't surprise you with unexpected blessings of joy, freedom, and grace.

**Week Two**

Take some time to examine your regular giving in prayer. If you do not have a set amount that you give, make that change this week. Set up automatic recurring giving to your local church or a charity you believe in. Start with an amount that makes a difference, something you will miss. If you do regularly give, challenge yourself to increase your current giving or begin additional gifts to somewhere new. Remember that everything you have is a gift from God, and train your heart by choosing to give back first. Trust that he will take care of you as a good Father does.

Another approach is to take a look at your expenses through the lens of someone who is very poor, who can only afford the necessities. Categorize your expenses in two ways: the things you must have—basic food, clothing, shelter—and the things you enjoy having—subscriptions, nice dinners out, extra clothing, trips, and so on. Then, challenge yourself to budget more money to give to others than you spend on the nonessential things that are just for you. Train your heart to consider others who are without basic needs when you are spending on the extra.

Pray for each member of your group by name each week.

## In Community

*Group Prayer Prompts*

**Week One:** Spend five minutes in silence together, asking God to reveal areas in your life where you have not been generous or have made money, comfort, security, or success an idol. Share these things, and then have one group member pray for a heart of generosity for all.

**Week Two:** Have someone in the group pray for a spirit of generosity for the church as a whole in the giving of both their finances and their time to meaningful ministries.

*Group Discussion*

**Week One**

1. What stood out to you in the chapter and/or the Scripture readings?
2. Who have you known or observed in your life that you would consider radically generous?
3. What inspired them to live this way?

**Week Two**

1. How did the week one practice of generosity go? Share some of your experiences.
2. Have you experienced freedom in giving in your life in any way, big or small?
3. Is there something God has put on your heart that you need to give up to follow him in the way you give?
4. If you had a chance to get into the Go Deeper material, what stood out to you?

## Go Deeper

"A Generous Gospel: The New Testament Themes Part 4," *Exploring My Strange Bible* podcast, Tim Mackie

Testing God, a sermon series by Jonathan Storment of the Pleasant Valley Church of Christ in Little Rock, Arkansas, Fall 2024

"For the Sake of Others: For the Sake of the Poor," *Bridgetown Audio Podcast,* October 14, 2024

"Spiritual Transformation and Money," *Strengthening the Soul of Your Leadership* podcast, Ruth Haley Barton, season 9, episode 4

"Becoming a People of Generosity," sermon by John Mark Comer of the Bridgetown Church in Portland, Oregon

Generosity Practice, practicingtheway.org/generosity

For direct links, visit www.pvcc.org/resources.

## Practice Nine

# SERVING

FOR MANY YEARS, I STRUGGLED with what I would call a works-based faith. I wanted desperately to have a relationship with God, to really know him and feel his presence, but I knew deep down something was missing. I volunteered and served over and over, chasing what I thought would bring me closer to him.

And in many ways, it did. I felt God's call to foster care and have grown in love and empathy as we grew our family through adoption. This decision made a lasting impact on us as we have raised our kids to care for the most vulnerable, and it has provided a window into the heart of God in the way we are now called to love. Serving alongside others in my church and community in this ministry has brought so much joy and purpose, but deep down, something was still missing in my relationship with God.

Just like in the generosity practice, I needed to flip the script. I needed to start by seeking God and *then* let the love he had for me overflow as an offering I could pour out in service to others.

> For it is by grace you have been saved, through faith—and this is not from yourselves, it is the gift of God—not by works, so that no one can boast. For we are God's handiwork, created in Christ Jesus to do good works, which God prepared in advance for us to do. (Eph. 2:8–10)

Paul addresses human nature directly when he leads with grace in Ephesians 2:8–10. He is assuring us of the gift that is our salvation and reminding us that we cannot earn our spot at the table. Jesus has already prepared it for us. He also immediately adds that we were created to be on mission with God.

God wants us to partner with him in renewing his world and bringing heaven to earth. He has prepared us with unique giftings and passions and will equip us along the way. When we follow Jesus's example, seeking first to be fully known and loved by God, our acts of service overflow from the love that we have received. Our efforts become beautiful offerings of love that can fill us up instead of wearing us out.

### The Joy of Interruption

Throughout the Gospels, we find Jesus on his way to a meal, to be alone with God, or to teach when he is interrupted by someone in need. One of the most famous of these times is found in Matthew 9:20–22 (also in Mark 5:25–34 and Luke 8:43–48). Jesus is on his way to heal the twelve-year-old daughter of Jairus, an official of the synagogue. The crowd is pressing in around him as he makes his way to Jairus's home.

A woman with great faith and great suffering has been looking for Jesus. She has been ill and an outcast for years and has heard a healer is near. She follows the crowd toward him until she gets close enough to reach out. Without a word exchanged, she touched him and was healed. That could've been the end of their encounter, and he could've hurried along to the next stop on his packed agenda, but Jesus is never in a hurry. He does not see interruptions as we do because he is not driven by pride, accomplishments, or guilt. Love is his motivation. His mission is not about how much he can get done but about who he can reach.

Jesus only had a few years to change the course of human history. His mission was huge, and his timeline was tight. The lessons he was teaching would need to be learned so well by his followers that they could be replicated for generations. I think it's safe to say he was busier than we are. And yet he always takes the time to see and to serve those who need him. Over and over, he patiently responds with compassion and humility. Jesus modeled that serving others does not need to wait for a season where we have margin. He repeatedly illustrated that the heart of God, and great joy, is found in taking the time to be interrupted to serve others.

## Compassion

Jesus, in his times of prayer, fasting, silence, solitude, and forgiveness, has prepared his heart, mind, soul, and body to serve God by serving others. He is confident and assured in his identity as God's son. Because he rests, trusts, and finds his faith in God, he is free to live into a posture of compassion for the weak and the broken.

As his followers, we can also walk so closely with the Father that we reflect Jesus in how we are bearing with others, meeting them where they are, and bringing healing and comfort. And in serving others, our hearts become more and more transformed in his likeness.

**Read and Meditate on**
Matthew 14:6–21
Read it slowly a couple of times, placing yourself in the roles of Jesus, the disciples, and the crowd.

We know that Jesus was fully human and loved John very much. At this moment, he was feeling the full weight of his humanity as he learned about his cousin's gruesome and senseless death. He was looking for a place to be alone with God to receive comfort. Jesus pulled up to shore and realized he was not alone. A crowd of thousands had gathered and were expecting to be healed. How easy would it have been for Jesus to just say, "Nope. Not today."? How easy and understandable would it have been for him to just disappear for a little while? After all, he needed time with his Father, to rest and grieve, and those people would still need him in the morning.

But his character is always love, and in compassion, he stopped and began to heal them.

The disciples, who joined Jesus as the day wore on, had watched him love people this way for a year. Day after day as they followed him, the disciples began to be changed by the way Jesus treated everyone. As they walked with him, they not only witnessed this amazing love but they had been called into it. How could you not want to be more like this man who loved others so well?

While Jesus was still with the crowd, *they* realized the people were hungry. The disciples took their concern to Jesus. Their strategies and faith were not perfect, but they were growing in love. They brought Jesus a small plate of bread and fish, presumably even a little embarrassed by the smallness of the gesture, but not sure what else to do. They brought what they had and then got to participate in one of the greatest miracles ever recorded.

Jesus is asking the same of us as disciples in our context. He is asking us to watch him, and in love for others, bring him our small offering of time, talent, and passion so he can bless and multiply it.

**Read and Meditate on**
Matthew 20:25–28; Luke 9:46–48; John 13:14–17

## Humility

Jesus's disciples, like us, wanted to know where they stood. Who is the greatest? Who is really getting it, who does the rabbi like the best, who will be the leader? Spoiler alert: None of them were the greatest, you are not the greatest, and neither am I. Even when we are self-aware and self-confident enough to know and be okay with this, we still don't want to be the least, right? No one wants to be the last to get what they want, the last to be considered, the last to be respected, or the last to be heard.

As Jesus and his disciples gathered to celebrate the Passover in John 13, it's easy to relate to their situation. They were hungry, their feet were dirty, and they sat waiting because washing feet was a servant's job. They probably wondered why the servant was late or blamed the host for not making sure this important pre-dinner task was taken care of.

Before we get too down on these guys, put yourself in their sandals. If I were to pick up that towel, it could permanently affect my place in the group, and foot-washing is not where my talents and passion lie. What if because I did it this time, they expect me to do it the next time? What if I miss an important teaching or a chance to impress Jesus with my understanding while I'm out filling the bowl with water? Or worse, what if I'm no longer taken seriously because the other guys begin to see me as their servant? I have much more to offer than making sure everyone's feet are clean.

But Jesus redefines all of our roles. Not only did Jesus take the lowest possible position, but he took that posture in the midst of an ordinary rhythm in their lives. Jesus did not take his followers on a special trip or to a special place to teach them to serve. He showed them how to live in a radically humble posture of service no matter where they were.

Trips, events, and programs that give us opportunities to serve with our communities and families are wonderfully formative. But we can't forget their purpose is to form us into people who humbly serve in everyday life. The measuring stick for a life formed by service is how well you love the people who know you the best and are around you the most. Richard Foster points out in *Celebration of Discipline* that, in discipleship to King Jesus, "the spiritual authority of Jesus is an authority not found in a person or a title, but in a towel."[1]

Foster also explains how intentionally making service part of your everyday lifestyle grows humility more than any other practice or discipline. When we let go of our pride and let Jesus control our lives, we grow in the grace of humility and have room for the freedom, love, and peace that come from being the least. When we have chosen this position, we don't have to worry about being taken advantage of, manipulated, or devalued.

When we serve in secret and in the lowest of ways, we push back harder and harder on the human desire for honor and recognition and begin to crucify our pride and arrogance. We choose to become available and vulnerable, fully surrendering our rights as servants to Christ.

**Witness**

As John 13 continues to unfold, we come across some of the most famous words of Jesus: "By this everyone will know that you are my disciples, if you love one another" (13:35). You don't have to be part of a church very long before you notice that most Western Christian people struggle with evangelism. The word carries a unique form of baggage piled on by anyone from street preachers with megaphones to televangelists to well-intentioned sermons that leave you feeling guilty but still ill-equipped and uninspired to share your faith.

**Read and Meditate on**
John 13:31–34; 1 Peter 3:13–16

We never really know how people will respond if we share our faith, so for too many times we just keep silent. But Jesus meets us where we are. He shows us over and over that when we simply decide to love the people around us well, no matter what, we get more and more opportunities to share the hope that we have (1 Pet. 3:15).

The more we step out and love in ways that the world around us thinks is crazy, the more opportunity we have to share why we would do such a thing in the first place.

**Individual Practice**

Pray for each member of your group by name each week.

**Week One:** Every morning in the coming week, before your feet hit the floor, pray: "Father God, bring me someone I can serve today and increase my love for you and others." And when you are thanked for what you do, just tell them it is nothing compared to the love you have received from God. Then each night, reflect on the (big or small) ways God answered that prayer and how you responded.

**Week Two:** Spend some time praying about areas where you are lacking compassion and humility. Who are you reluctant to serve? Who are you resentful of? Practice praying for ways to serve those people or people groups and ask God to increase your love for them.

### In Community

*Group Prayer Prompts*

**Week One:** Check in with each other and give any life updates or personal prayer requests. Spend a few minutes in silence asking the Holy Spirit to reveal needs in your community. Pray together for the vulnerable, with each member covering a different need or people group that is on their heart.

**Week Two:** Check in with each other and give any life updates or personal prayer requests. Someone volunteer to bring a list of ministries your church is involved in or pull them up on your church's website. Pass the list around, praying over each one.

*Group Discussion*

**Week One**

1. What stood out to you in the chapter and/or the Scripture readings?
2. "Whoever wants to be my disciple must deny themselves and take up their cross and follow me. For whoever wants to save their life will lose it, but whoever loses their life for

me will find it" (Matt. 16:24–25). What does it mean to lose your life and then find it? Is there someone in your life who has done this well?

3. A minister friend of mine frequently says, "When you are climbing the ladder of success, you will meet Jesus on your way down." We see this in Jesus's life, but Christians usually still celebrate success and ambition as much as our culture does. How do you reconcile these two truths as a disciple-maker?
4. How often do you seek God's direction in prayer for whom you should serve and how? How does this approach differ from simply always responding to the requests being made in your church or community?

**Week Two**

1. How did the week one practice of serving go? Share some of your experiences.
2. Share a time when serving in a particular role or area left you feeling worn out and a time when it filled you up. What do you think made the difference?
3. The entire Bible tells of God's heart for the vulnerable. When we serve as Jesus did, without regard to background or circumstance and without condition, we are free to grow in the grace of humility. What about this is most challenging? Who do you find it hard to serve?
4. If you had a chance to get into the Go Deeper material, what stood out to you?

## Go Deeper

"Empower & Equip: Making a Difference Isn't Complicated," *The Christine Cain Podcast,* season 1, episode 225

*Visions of Vocation: Common Grace for the Common Good,* Steven Garber

*Seeking God: Finding Another Kind of Life with St. Ignatius and Dallas Willard,* Trevor Hudson, Chapter 6

"Service," featuring Bethany Allen, *John Mark Comer Teachings* podcast, Unforced Rhythms of Grace E7

For direct links, visit www.pvcc.org/resources.

# Practice Ten

# RULE OF LIFE

THE TERM *RULE OF LIFE* has been used over the centuries to describe intentionally organizing your life around practicing the spiritual habits or disciplines modeled by Jesus. Having a spiritual rule of life simply means you consider what exposes you most to God's love, making you more like Jesus, and then plan how you will intentionally pursue those habits in your daily, weekly, and annual routines. None of us drift toward disciple-making, and a rule of life helps to ensure that our schedule aligns with our values.

**Read and Meditate on**
Deuteronomy 4:9; Matthew 7:24–27; 2 Timothy 1:6–9

Practicing a rule of life traces back to the early monastic movement in the fourth century. St. Benedict wrote the most well-known rule in the sixth century, and it has influenced Eastern and Western Christians for roughly fifteen hundred years.

Benedict's rule was written for the monastic movement, but it remains timeless in that most of it is applicable to life outside a monastery. It deals with qualities we see in the life of Jesus, and it expresses what we all need for a full life as a disciple: humility, patience, simplicity, solitude, caring for others, and living in community. Benedict's rule offers people a plan for living a balanced, simple, and prayerful life, and it is still used today by every Benedictine monastery and convent in the world.

If the word "rule" sounds too legalistic and maybe a bit intimidating, take a breath, because you already have one. Even if it's not written down, we all have regular rhythms in our lives that are forming who we are as people. Like a trellis or a fence with vines growing along it, the structure of our days, weeks, and months forms who we are. So the question is not, "Will you adopt a rule of life?" but rather, "What is your rule of life, and what kind of person is it shaping you into?"

Moving toward intentional spiritual habits by creating a rule of life ensures we keep God at the center of everything we do. Like the choice to pursue a life as a disciple-maker, the starting point of any rule of life is a desire to be with God and love him.

## Sample Rules

Like all the other practices we've covered, a rule of life is a gift when used as it is intended, and there is no one way to do it. Grace abounds for your rule to differ from the others in your group based on your personality, season of life, and stage of discipleship to Jesus. Know yourself, and don't feel pressure to fit into someone else's rhythm. Start where you are, give yourself grace, and move forward with Jesus.

### *John's Rule*

*John is a shepherd in his church and a top-level executive at work. His rule is simple, but the effects on his heart and community are anything but.*

**DAILY**

- Upon waking: Spend 15 minutes in silence with God
- Midday: Pray the Lord's Prayer
- Evening: Read a short passage of Scripture and reflect on the day

**WEEKLY**

- Practice Sabbath every Sunday
- Do one unexpected act of kindness each week for a friend or stranger
- Reach out to one person not in my normal circle in some way (send a text or card, pray for them and let them know, invite someone over or out)
- Attend a small group

**MONTHLY**

- Serve food at the homeless shelter
- Meet a need in my church
- Plan a half day to spend alone with God

---

*Amy's Rule*

*Amy is a young mom and has a mid-level job in a small office. She keeps her rule on a note card in her car to remind and reorient herself often. She has ups and downs in her faith journey and feels that her weekly Sabbath is the best place to reconnect with God, even when it doesn't go as planned.*

**DAILY**

- Time of silence each morning, or breath prayer
- Meditate on Scripture each morning, let God speak
- Pray over the day's schedule each morning

- Watch for tension, stress, or frustration, as signs that my heart needs to be reoriented toward God
- Check email at designated times throughout the workday to limit distraction
- Take regular breaks for prayer, silence, and refocusing on God's presence and goodness
- Pray a prayer of examen over the day each evening
- Pray with spouse for each child

**WEEKLY**

- Worship gathering with my faith community
- Time in small group
- Fast on Friday
- Sabbath on Saturday

**MONTHLY/ANNUALLY**

- Plan intentional times of rest beyond weekly Sabbath; retreats—for a weekend or just a day to focus on God
- Plan intentional dates with spouse and each kid

---

*Roger and Mandy's Rule*

*Roger and Mandy have been married for thirty-two years. They are newly retired and wrote their rule together as a way to focus this next season of life on God and to keep each other accountable. They are much busier than they ever dreamed they'd be during retirement and have found their rule essential to grounding their lives in God and his mission for them in this season.*

**GOAL ONE:** Begin and end each day with a slow pace with God

- One hour of quiet time each morning
- Turn off phone one hour before bed

- Make sure to get eight hours of sleep each night

**GOAL TWO:** Grow in community
- Invite someone to lunch once per week
- Host a meal with family, friends, or neighbors once a week
- Attend a small group
- Serve in a group ministry at church

**GOAL THREE:** Connect deeper with God
- Pause every afternoon to pray a psalm
- Journal prayers each night
- Experience different worship types and formats

SAMPLE WORKSHEETS

# My Rule of Life

**How will I connect with God:**

*Daily:*

*Weekly:*

*Monthly:*

**Annual Goals:**

## Rule of Life Worksheet

| | Spiritual: Love God with Heart and Soul | Physical: Love God with Strength | Intellectual: Love God with Mind | Family: Love One Another | Community: Love Neighbor As Self |
|---|---|---|---|---|---|
| DAILY | | | | | |
| WEEKLY | | | | | |
| MONTHLY | | | | | |
| QUARTERLY | | | | | |
| YEARLY | | | | | |

### How to Begin Writing Your Rule

Ask God for guidance in putting together a rhythm that will meet your desire for a life-giving connection with him and authentic spiritual formation. Before you put pen to paper, spend a few days just praying for these things.

*Reflect on the Time Spent with Each Practice*

What has worked best for you to achieve connection and formation during this study and throughout your life? Also, consider which practices are particularly needed to address a pattern of sin you struggle with in your current lifestyle.

Consider what kind of person you want to be. What do you want to be known for, and what kind of influence do you want to have?

*Begin Writing Your Plan*

Put pen to paper and create a draft. Start with goals for just this season of life, whether that is based on your current life stage or the actual season of the year if your schedule changes with the school year or physical seasons.

Ask yourself:

- What practices will you use?
- Where and when will you do each practice (daily, monthly, yearly)?
- How will others be incorporated for encouragement, accountability, and discipleship?
- How do you need to adjust your schedule to make this happen? Who in your life needs to know about this to make sure you can make it happen?

*Take a Break*

Put your rule aside for a few days. Pray, and rest in God's presence. Then come back. Is it realistic? Does it meet the purpose? Is it personal and specific enough?

*Commit and Adjust*

Commit yourself prayerfully out of a desire for God, not a sense of obligation to follow your rule. Continue to adjust, experiment, and evaluate with God in each season of life.

### Individual Practice

Create a draft of your rule of life to share with the group, then continue working on it, living in it, and adjusting it in the following week and in each season of life and stage of discipleship.

Pray for each member of your group by name.

## In Community

*Group Prayer Prompt*

Spend ten or so minutes in silent meditation thinking over the practices studied: Community, Prayer, Reading and Meditating on Scripture, Silence and Solitude, Fasting, Sabbath, Confessing and Forgiving, Generosity, and Serving. Give the Spirit time to nudge you toward areas that brought you closer to God and helped counter specific sins in your life. Discuss what practices stood out.

*Group Discussion*

1. What stood out to you in the chapter and/or the Scripture readings?
2. Be completely honest with yourself and your group. In this season of your life, what types of priorities and activities are running your rule of life, and what kind of a person is it shaping you into?
3. Writing goals and resolutions are commonplace in our culture. What makes the process of creating a rule of life different?
4. What did you find most challenging about creating your rule?
5. When will you need to check in to make adjustments to your rule, and what will you put in place to make sure this happens (i.e., a reminder on your calendar, accountability within the group, and so on)?

## Go Deeper

*Unhurrying with a Rule of Life*, nine-lesson series with Practicing the Way

*Rule of Life Workbook* (pdf) and Rule of Life Builder, Practicing the Way

For direct links, visit www.pvcc.org/resources.

# WHAT'S NEXT? MULTIPLY

IF WE ARE NOT INTENTIONAL about multiplication, spiritual formation can become just about us and our relationship with God. An old song by Amy Grant keeps coming to my mind on this topic. It was on a cassette tape my parents had when I was young, and the words have never left me. The song was called "Mountain Top," and it is about the joy and peace of being with God on the mountain of the Lord. The last half of the chorus sings, "I've got to come down from that mountain top to the people in the valley below, or they'll never know that they can go to the mountain of the Lord."

As tempting as it can be to only dive deeper and deeper into a relationship with God, disciples are called to look outward. We must remember that the practices are about the *how*. Our *why* is for the sake of others.

> For the sake of others. That is the aim and destination of all spiritual formation in the way of Jesus. It's not personal wellness or self-care or work-life balance or even character formation. All of that is a part of it, but it's more like the collateral of following Jesus. The tip of the spear is giving my life away in sacrificial, other-centered love.
>
> **—Tyler Stayton,** "You Know a Tree by Its Fruit"[1]

Stayton has a wonderful lesson on this included in the Going Deeper section. In it, he cautions his church to not let the *how* of spiritual formation—the way we read the Bible or pray, honor the Sabbath, or live out any other practice—outrun the *why* of spiritual formation. This, according to Stayton, is de-forming as the practice is drained of its power. When we live in the how and not the why, "we become rigid instead of free, uptight instead of at peace, angry instead of gentle, repelling instead of inviting." Because we are measuring our spiritual health by the wrong instrument, we think we are healthy, but we are getting sicker and sicker by the day.

We see this idea all over the Gospels, especially in the stories of Jesus healing on the Sabbath. Matthew records in 12:1–13 that Jesus was criticized twice on the same Sabbath day: once for picking grain to eat as they walked along and again just a few moments later for pausing in the synagogue long enough to heal a man who had come to worship and had a crippled hand. The reaction in both stories shows that the practice of Sabbath had de-formed the critics of Jesus. In their personal lives, Sabbath had become an excuse not to help others, to the point that when Jesus came along, it was easy for them to turn it into a trap. Satan will use any tool, even our desire for spiritual formation, to turn our hearts away from God.

### Yes, You Are Ready

Jesus's ministry depended on the intentional multiplication of disciples. Now that this study has come to an end, what is your next step in your path to disciple-making? Whether God is leading you to start a new discipling group when this one ends, branch out into a new area of service, mentor youth in your church or community, or teach these practices to your children and work on them with your own family, disciples make disciples. It is in the very definition we began with Jesus's words in Matthew 4:19: "Come, follow me," Jesus said, "and I will show you how to fish for people" (NLT).

- **Be with Jesus** (*Come, follow me*): Choose him. Abide in him. Slow down enough to hear his voice and practice being in his presence.
- **Become like Jesus** (*I will show you how*): Allow the Holy Spirit to transform your heart and help you become a person of deep love, a person to whom the teachings of Jesus are second nature. You will not get everything "right" all the time, but over time your will and your heart will become aligned with his.
- **Do what Jesus did** (*Fish for people*): What would Jesus do with your one and only life if he were walking around in your skin today? How would he interact with your neighbors and family, answer your emails, and connect in your community?

---

Therefore go and make disciples of all nations, baptizing them in the name of the Father and of the Son and of the Holy Spirit, and teaching them to obey everything I have commanded you. And surely I am with you always, to the very end of the age. (Matt. 28:19–20)

---

These words of Jesus have famously been called the Great Commission. They are Jesus's last words to the eleven in Matthew, as they gather together for the last time in person on a hillside. Can you imagine what Jesus must have felt, leaving the world's fate in their hands after just a few short years and all they have been through together? This idea gets even more unreal when you back up to verse 17: "When they saw him, they worshipped him; but some doubted."

Some doubted. Every contextual clue here points to this being a scene with just the eleven disciples, not a crowd. This means that even in this holy space of Jesus's last interaction, there was doubt that he was who he said he was. Even among the eleven who walked with him day in and day out, learning how to know God and obey what he wants for their lives, there was doubt. Even after seeing him walk on water, raise the dead, heal the sick, and calm the storm, and even after putting their fingers in the nail holes in his hands, some doubted.

Maybe it was too much for the disciples to take in and process. Maybe the trauma of the crucifixion was still too raw and painful to fully move on just yet. Maybe they could not accept how good God really was and just felt it was too good to be true. Regardless of the reason, Jesus trusted them. In their doubt, in the uncertainty of their ability or knowledge, in their unique strengths and weaknesses, Jesus commissioned them to make new disciples.

All they had to do was tell the world about him and share his love.

And that is all we have to do today. If you feel inadequate or unsure of how or even why you should share this story of Jesus, you are not alone. It can be helpful to start at the beginning and simply reflect on what God has done for you.

### Fifteen-Second Testimony

The fifteen-second testimony is so powerful because it demonstrates that God has the power to change our lives! It is a story of contrasts between our old and new lives in Christ. This method makes it easy to tell your story using four simple words or phrases.

You will note that this is a very scripted method, but this is done purposely to keep you on track and to avoid getting wordy. The more comfortable you get with it, the more you will be able to say it naturally and adapt it to any situation.

Begin with these three simple steps:

- Think of TWO WORDS that describe your life before you met Jesus.
- Think of TWO WORDS that describe how Jesus changed your life.
- Then share as follows: "There was a time in my life when I was (insecure) and (angry). Then I met Jesus, trusted him, and made him number one in my life. Now I am (secure) and (full of joy). Do you have a story like this?"

Practice this method in a group, use that last phrase to pass it along to someone else to practice . . . and so on.

If you became a believer at a young age and don't remember your life before Jesus, think of two words describing a time of crisis, a period of uncertainty, or a faith struggle you have been through. Then omit the phrase "I met Jesus" and just say, "Then I put my trust in Jesus and made him number one in my life." Make it work for your situation. Most importantly, practice it and see if you can naturally share it with unbelievers and believers.

For those discipling children and youth, this process can also be applied to situations when a child is struggling through a big mistake they have made. After they have had time to confess and ask forgiveness, walk them through processing their growth and feelings using a format such as this: "There was a time this week when I felt ______ and _______ because I ________. Then Jesus forgave me, and now I am ______ and ________."

**Go Where?**

The local church I am blessed to serve has a long-standing history of global missions. It has been remarkable over the decades to see our church fully support families who have given their lives to preach the gospel around the world. It has been equally remarkable to work with volunteer members of our missions team here at home who want to help us all see that the mission field is as much across an ocean as it is across the street.

God has uniquely created you for the time and place you live. He may put a specific calling on your heart to make a big missional change in your life, but more often, he's nudging us to make small, intentional moves right now. The question is, are we listening and will we respond?

"Go into all the world" was not just meant for every geography but also for every vocation, neighborhood, and life stage. Don't wait for the next mission trip or special event or campaign your church is hosting. You can simply start by asking someone today—a friend, coworker, neighbor, or even waiter or waitress—if they have ever been invited to your church. If not, tell them why you love it and extend the invitation.

Praying for someone is another great way to open the door to deeper connection and conversation. This can begin just by putting your phone away when you are in public. Slow down and focus on those around you. Start looking people in the eye when you come in contact with them every day, and you will be surprised by what God can do in those short moments. Ask them something about themselves, and if you feel a connection being made, whether it's with a coworker, neighbor, barista, gas station attendant, or unhoused person, or it's with the guy behind you in a line, simply take it one step deeper and say, "I'd like to pray for you this week. Is there anything specific I can pray for in your life?" Remember that so many people we pass every day are starving for a real community and someone to see them. Jesus did that everywhere he went, and as his disciples, we certainly can, too.

## As You Go

Spiritual formation is not completed in a season with one study and then you are formed. It is a lifelong journey that involves continually shaping and adjusting your rule of life throughout each season, allowing the Holy Spirit to transform you into a person of deep love. It takes desire and commitment.

Approach it not as a process or assignment but as an invitation you accept in response to the overflow of the love God has for you and the difference he has made in your life. As you continue to be with and become like Jesus, how will you be on the mission of Jesus? Spend time in prayer over the questions below and write out your answers, pausing to let the Holy Spirit open your heart. Share your answers with your group. Be open and honest about how you feel and the challenges you face as a person who wants to follow Jesus more deeply.

- How have you grown as a disciple?
- What challenges did you face?
- Whom will you disciple?
- How will you live differently in relationships with others now?
- How will you intentionally share the gospel?

Need one more tangible next step? Invite one person from the group you have studied this book with, or a close friend if you have read it on your own, to fast and pray with you about starting a new group and whom you will invite. Let the Holy Spirit lead you in sharing what you have experienced with others. Each time you practice the ways of Jesus with others, they will come alive in your life in new ways. There is no limit to the depth of love and relationship God is offering. We just have to accept the invitation to follow.

## Go Deeper

"You Know a Tree by Its Fruit," *Bridgetown Audio Podcast*, For the Sake of Others series, September 23, 2024

"Who's Your One Training – Fifteen Second Testimony," Southeastern Seminary, YouTube video, February 28, 2020

Discipleship Self-Assessment, Pleasant Valley Church of Christ

Spiritual Health Reflection, Practicing the Way

For direct links, please visit www.pvcc.org/resources.

# ABOUT THE AUTHOR

Courtney Hirscheider is a mother to Lily, Jude, Evy, and Wyatt and wife to her best friend, Blake, who prompted the writing of this work. She serves as the Vision Strategies and Communications Minister at the Pleasant Valley Church of Christ in Little Rock, Arkansas. Courtney is passionate about growing as a disciple of Jesus and in relationship with God. She loves the outdoors, a good cup of black coffee, trips with R. S., and rides to nowhere in particular in her '78 Jeep CJ7.

# NOTES

## Introduction: Disciple-Making and Desire

1. Gerald Sittser, *Water from a Deep Well: Christian Spirituality from Early Martyrs to Modern Missionaries* (InterVarsity, 2010), 48.
1. Dallas Willard, *The Great Omission* (HarperOne, 2006), 8.
2. Jefferson Bethke and Jon Tyson, *Fighting Shadows: Overcoming 7 Lies That Keep Men from Becoming Fully Alive* (Thomas Nelson, 2024), 99.
3. Bethke and Tyson, *Fighting Shadows*, 100.
4. Ronald Rolheiser, *The Holy Longing: The Search for a Christian Spirituality* (Image, 2009), 24.
5. Trevor Hudson, *Seeking God: Finding Another Kind of Life with St. Ignatius and Dallas Willard* (NavPress, 2022), 42.

## Practice One: Community

1. "Community," Practicing the Way, https://practicingthewayarchives.org/practices/community.
2. Aristides, *The Apology of Aristides*, ed. J. Armitage Robinson (Cambridge University Press, 1891), chapter 15, https://www.tertullian.org/fathers/aristides_05_trans.htm.
3. Vivek Murthy, "Work and the Loneliness Epidemic," *Harvard Business Review*, September 26, 2017, https://hbr.org/2017/09/work-and-the-loneliness-epidemic.

4. John Mark Comer, host, John Mark Comer Teachings, May 13, 2022, "Radically Ordinary Hospitality: Eating and Drinking Ep 1," Practicing the Way, 57 min.

5. Rosaria Butterfield, *The Gospel Comes with a House Key: Practicing Radically Ordinary Hospitality in Our Post-Christian World* (Crossway, 2018), 11.

6. Robin Dunbar, *How Many Friends Does One Person Need? Dunbar's Number and Other Evolutionary Quirks* (Harvard University Press, 2010).

## Practice Two: Prayer

1. Dallas Willard, *The Great Omission: Reclaiming Jesus's Essential Teachings on Discipleship* (HarperCollins, 2006), 125.

2. Ruth Haley Barton, *Sacred Rhythms: Arranging Our Lives for Spiritual Transformation* (InterVarsity, 2006), 63.

3. Sheridan Voysey, "The Breath Prayer," July 28, 2021, https://www.sheridanvoysey.com/breathprayer/.

4. Pete Greig, "Power of Prayer: For the Sake of Others," sermon at Bridgetown Church in Portland, Oregon, September 29, 2024, https://www.youtube.com/watch?v=tdjbbZfjAZM.

5. Brother Lawrence, *The Practice of the Presence of God* (Whitaker House, 1982), 38.

6. Ronald Rolheiser, *Prayer: Our Deepest Longing* (Franciscan Media, 2013), preface.

## Practice Three: Scripture

1. Ruth Haley Barton, *Sacred Rhythms: Arranging Our Lives for Spiritual Transformation* (InterVarsity, 2006), 50.

2. Anthony Schmidt, "Slave Bible from the 1800s Omitted Key Passages That Could Incite Rebellion," interview by Michel Martin, *All Things Considered*, NPR, December 9, 2018, audio, https://www.npr.org/transcripts/674995075.

## Practice Four: Silence and Solitude

1. Ruth Haley Barton, *Sacred Rhythms: Arranging Our Lives for Spiritual Transformation* (InterVarsity, 2006), 32.

2. Ruth Haley Barton, *Invitation to Silence and Solitude* (InterVarsity, 2004), 19.

3. Sue McGreevey, "Eight Weeks to a Better Brain," *Harvard Gazette*, January 21, 2011, https://news.harvard.edu/gazette/story/2011/01/eight-weeks-to-a-better-brain/.

4. Henri Nouwen, "Solitude Is the Place of Conversion," Henri Nouwen Society, May 29, 2024, https://henrinouwen.org/meditations/solitude-is-the-place-of-conversion/.

5. Ruth Haley Barton, "Solitude: In God for the World," Transforming Center, August 2015, https://transformingcenter.org/2015/08/solitude-sake-others/.

## Practice Five: Fasting

1. This idea of speaking only where the Bible speaks finds its home in proposition five of Thomas Campbell's *Declaration and Address of the Christian Association of Washington*, printed by Brown and Sample, 1809, https://webfiles.acu.edu/departments/Library/HR/restmov_nov11/www.mun.ca/rels/restmov/texts/tcampbell/da/DA-1ST.HTM.

2. Thomas Tarrants, "The Place of Fasting in the Christian Life," C. S. Lewis Institute, June 6, 2018, https://www.cslewisinstitute.org/resources/the-place-of-fasting-in-the-christian-life/.

3. Richard Foster, *Celebration of Discipline: The Path to Spiritual Growth* (HarperOne, 2018), 47.

4. Gretchen Ronnevik, *Ragged: Spiritual Disciplines for the Spiritually Exhausted* (1517 Publishing, 2021), 150.

5. "The Fasting Practice," Practicing the Way, practicingtheway.org/fasting.

6. Anna Dewdney, *Llama Llama Holiday Drama* (Viking Books for Young Readers, 2010).

7. Foster, *Celebration of Discipline*, 55.

## Practice Six: Sabbath

1. John Ortberg, *The Life You've Always Wanted: Participant's Guide* (Zondervan, 2024), 42.
2. Beth Guckenberger, *Throw the First Punch: Defeating the Enemy Hell-Bent on Your Destruction* (David C. Cook, 2022), 137.
3. John Mark Comer, host, John Mark Comer Teachings, July 26, 2024, "Stop, Rest, Delight, Worship: Sabbath E4 Revamped," Practicing the Way, 55 min.
4. Ruth Haley Barton, *Sacred Rhythms: Arranging Our Lives for Spiritual Transformation* (InterVarsity, 2006).
5. Ruth Haley Barton, host, *Strengthening the Soul of Your Leadership*, season 17, episode 6, "Sharing Sabbath Presence within Our Families," October 4, 2022, 57:39.
6. John Mark Comer and guests, "Sabbath 01, 02, 03, and 04," *Rule of Life* (podcast), Practicing the Way, 2022.
7. Andy Crouch, *The Tech-Wise Family: Everyday Steps for Putting Technology in Its Proper Place* (Baker Books, 2017); Jonathan Haidt, *The Anxious Generation* (Penguin Press, 2024).

## Practice Seven: Confession and Forgiveness

1. Beth Guckenberger, *Throw the First Punch: Defeating the Enemy Hell-Bent on Your Destruction* (David C. Cook, 2022), 136.
2. Trevor Hudson, *Seeking God: Finding Another Kind of Life with St. Ignatius and Dallas Willard* (NavPress, 2022), 50.
3. Tyler Staton, "For the Sake of Others: How Many Times Should I Forgive?," sermon at Bridgetown Church in Portland, Oregon, November 18, 2024, https://www.youtube.com/watch?v=9ss5GsyXvk8.
4. Dietrich Bonhoeffer, *Life Together: The Classic Exploration of Christian in Community* (HarperOne, 2009), 116.

### Practice Eight: Generosity

1. Tyler Staton, "For the Sake of Others: For the Sake of the Poor," sermon at Bridgetown Church in Portland, Oregon, October 14, 2024, https://www.youtube.com/watch?v=RsdHsLfpCXI.

2. Miguel Echevarria, "John," in *The New Testament in Color: A Multiethnic Bible Commentary*, ed. Esau McCaulley, Janette H. Ok, Osvaldo Padilla, and Amy Peeler (InterVarsity, 2024), 237.

3. John Mark Comer, "Becoming a People of Generosity," sermon at Bridgetown Church in Portland, Oregon, October 13, 2019, https://bridgetown.church/teachings-vision-series-2019/becoming-people-of-generosity.

4. "Getting Paid in America," payroll.org survey results, 2023, https://info.payroll.org/pdfs/npw/2023_Getting_Paid_In_America_survey_results.pdf.

5. Emily Batdorf, "Living Paycheck to Paycheck Statistics 2024," Forbes.com, updated April 2, 2024, https://www.forbes.com/advisor/banking/living-paycheck-to-paycheck-statistics-2024/.

6. Tim Mackie, host, New Testament Themes series, episode 4, "A Generous Gospel," The Bible Project, September 6, 2017, 55 min., https://bibleproject.com/podcast/generous-gospel-new-testament-themes-part-4.

### Practice Nine: Serving

1. Richard Foster, *Celebration of Discipline: The Path to Spiritual Growth* (HarperOne, 2018), 148.

### What's Next? Multiply

1. Tyler Staton, "For the Sake of Others: You Know a Tree by Its Fruit," sermon at Bridgetown Church in Portland, Oregon, September 23, 2024, https://www.youtube.com/watch?v=grlRvQymBEY.